MY THERAPIST'S DOG

MY THERAPIST'S DOG

Lessons in
Unconditional Love

DIANA WELLS

ALGONQUIN BOOKS OF

CHAPEL HILL

2004

Published by
ALGONQUIN BOOKS OF CHAPEL HILL
Post Office Box 2225
Chapel Hill, North Carolina 27515-2225

a division of
Workman Publishing
708 Broadway
New York, New York 10003

Library of Congress Cataloging-in-Publication Data
Wells, Diana, 1940–
My therapist's dog : lessons in unconditional love / Diana
Wells.—1st ed.
p. cm.
Includes bibliographical references.
ISBN 1-56512-371-9
1. Dogs—Therapeutic use.   2. Dogs—Psychological
aspects.   3. Dog owners—Psychology.   4. Human-animal
relationships.   5. Wells, Diana, 1940–   I. Title.
RM931.D63W456 2004
155.9'37—dc22   2003070911

10 9 8 7 6 5 4 3 2 1
First Edition

ACKNOWLEDGMENTS

First, as always, I thank my family for everything I hold most dear. Thank you to my good friends at Algonquin Books, especially Amy Gash for her unfailing enthusiasm and patience, as well as her editorial skills. Once again, I thank the staff of the Krauskopf Memorial Library for their help and friendship. I thank Susan Apollon for her kind encouragement, and Pat Stone, editor of *Greenprints,* who believed in my writing a dozen years ago. Above all, I thank all the dogs in my life, who loved me much more than I deserved, and without whom this book would not have been possible.

Note: This is a true story, but all the names in it, except those of my own dogs, have been changed. Some of the episodes in this book appeared, in a different form, in *Greenprints* magazine.

For Nemo. But all who mourn.

Thou saist thou art as weary as a dogge,
As angry, sick, and hungry as a dogge,
As dull and melancholy as a dogge,
As lazie, sleepie, idle as a dogge.
But why dost thou compare thee to a dogge?
In that, for which all men despise a dogge,
I will compare thee better to a dogge.
Thou art as faire and comely as a dogge,
Thou art as true and honest as a dogge,
Thou art as kinde and liberall as a dogge,
Thou art as wise and valiant as a dogge.

—SIR JOHN DAVIES, "In Cineam," c. 1595

CONTENTS

MY THERAPIST'S DOG

Dog-Tired

A T FIRST I DIDN'T KNOW, or care, if she had a dog. Exhausted with grief, I sat in her office and cried. And she handed me tissues, one by one.

I had been raised to distrust all forms of counseling. "Psychologists," my mother had said firmly, "pontificate. And their breath smells." My mother was English and my father Scottish. A "stiff upper lip" was very much a part of my upbringing. Anyway, in our family we considered ourselves too intelligent for any mental assistance: We could outwit anybody, and would soon have *them* on the couch instead. We thought of therapy as a kind of intellectual game. We were smart enough, we believed, to solve any problems that came our way.

But not devastation. Not my son and my sister dying

within a few weeks of each other. My sister had loved me since before I could remember, and I had thought that my son would be with us forever. So it was that both my past and my future seemed annihilated with one blow. Intellect has nothing to do with devastation. Because I had nowhere else to go, I went to a therapist.

I was acquainted with Beth when I first sought her out, because she had been the psychologist at my son Robin's school, and known him when he got in trouble. I think I first went to her hoping for some contact with Robin. Maybe she could tell me about him, fill in gaps between him and me, make him seem a bit nearer, now that he was gone? I had expected to visit her a couple of times to talk about Robin. But that wasn't what happened. I sat crying on her sofa, and she silently handed me tissues. She assumed at once that I would come back the next week, and the week after. She said, with firm gentleness, that I needed her help.

The dog came up later. At that time I never could have dreamed that her dog would do so much to link me with life again. Because it seemed that grief would never stop. Not very long after I began seeing Beth, my nephew, my father, my mother, and both my stepparents also died, one after another. I went to Beth in desperation and we had no medical insurance at the time, so I worried how we could pay her. She offered me the gift of her compassion, and said I need not pay her.

Perhaps, apart from my need of her, she had more than mere professional empathy toward me. I knew from friends of friends that her own son was, like Robin, brilliantly clever, but not always helped by this; it set him apart from his contemporaries. But although they might have been similar, her son was alive, and Robin was dead. Her son was in college. My son had found life so hard he had killed himself when he was only twenty-four.

And Beth knew about older sisters. I had had one, Anna, who had died of cancer shortly after Robin's suicide. But she had two, as I discovered, with whom she was very close. Sometimes she went away, and it would turn out that she had been with one or the other of her sisters, or the three of them had been on a trip together. Maybe she also saw in me another mother, another sister, less blessed than herself. Whatever her reason for taking me on, I gratefully accepted her charity because I had no choice.

I wanted, though, to do something for her in return. That was where the dog came in. I discovered about him after she had been away on vacation, and jealously I asked her if she was "sorry to be back." Childlike, I wanted her to say she was happy to be back, so she could see *me*. What she actually said was that she was sorry for her dog, because he so loved the beach. So I offered to take care of him if they went away again and couldn't take him along. Beth was ambivalent. She was always ambivalent when we touched on her personal life. It was a kind of dance—I was longing to know more, to be part of her cheery life, after offering up my own life in its bleak nakedness. She was handing me sedate little snippets, without emotion. She was side-stepping when I got too close. I was trying to make her part of what I had lost. She was about the same age as my dead sister. But she was not going to be *my* sister, except professionally.

Looking after her dog was another of these delicate dances. To let me care for him would be to allow participation in her life, a professional problem for her. On the other hand, it was also her husband's dog. He, she told me in that new language I was getting to know, had "bonded" with the dog, and mostly took care of him. If her husband agreed, maybe it would be a convenience for them. They would talk about it.

So it was that Luggs came into our lives. In the beginning her husband, whose name I learned was Paul, brought him to our house (no question of knowing where she lived—not professional!). It was a scorching hot afternoon when Paul first arrived with Luggs, who turned out to be a very large Labrador retriever. I had not thought to ask what breed of dog he was, and had expected something smaller, more manageable. Paul surprised me too. I had somehow imagined that most psychologists were married to men with gray beards. He did not have a gray beard. He did have strong opinions on how best to care for the dog. Luggs was to be fed twice a day and a cup was provided with which to measure the food (also provided). He was not to be let loose but kept inside, or walked. We would have a trial weekend and see how it went. Paul left.

I hadn't pictured this. I thought Luggs would be on vacation, frolicking outside with Nemo, our dog. Nemo was free to roam in the fields around our house, often returning with unspeakably horrible trophies. He didn't always eat his dog food, having, we presumed, ingested parts of the disgusting corpses. Sometimes he buried the gruesome remains of his prey, but more often he left the bodies on the lawn. On hot days these corpses swelled, then crawled with thousands of gorging maggots that hatched into huge, iridescent blue flies, veiling the corpse in musically humming circles. Nemo would lie beside this scene, waiting for the meat to ripen properly. He always looked faintly hurt when one of us would steel ourselves to remove the corpse, tossing it into a bramble thicket where Nemo couldn't get at it.

It was usually my husband, Richard, who undertook the corpse removal. I would pretend I hadn't (in spite of the smell) noticed it. Richard wasn't fooled by my pretense, but he was always nice about things like that. When we two had first met, I had one son and he had two, all about the same age. We made a new family. Not only did I bring him an extra little boy, but I was always adding new creatures to the household, which grew rapidly anyway because Richard and I had three more little boys together.

Robin was the first child we had between us, and for us he had some of the magic of a child first born to those who find love after much searching. It seemed as if, from the moment he was born, Robin never could live his life fast enough. He hardly slept. He walked when he was eight months old. He always knew exactly what he was going to do, and neither bribes nor threats could deflect him from his purpose.

ROBIN AND, TWO years later, his brother Chuck were born in Italy, where I first met Richard, a sculptor. We lived in a huge stone house on the top of a mountain, surrounded by marble quarries. I used to walk to the valley every morning to buy fresh produce. I carried down a small milk can, to be filled by an old woman with a huge milk can on the back of a rickety cart. Fish was sold in our village once a week, the fishmonger standing in the center of the square and singing out what was available that day. When I remarked that his voice sounded unusual to my ears, my neighbors said that wasn't surprising, because he came from the next town up the coast!

Richard spent his days carving marble. I stayed home with the children and various animals. When Chuck was born, I couldn't carry both babies down to the valley to shop, so I bought a donkey. Both little boys could fit on her back, and I hung baskets each side of her for the vegetables. The only problem was, she would turn and sneak a bite out of the baskets whenever she could. If I walked on her left, she snatched a vegetable out of the right-hand basket. If I moved to her right, she quickly grabbed a morsel from the left basket.

It was a happy time. It seemed that life, like the bright Mediterranean sun, shone down on us, and always would. We acquired kittens and hens and ducks, and a goat that had kids. I used to joke that I specialized in five varieties of manure, excluding the kind in the diapers (which I washed by hand and hung in the sun to dry), but I didn't mind. I loved Italy. When the goat was ill and the vet came and saw to her, I asked how much I owed him. He said, "Signora, that is between me and the goat." But when the cat was ill, he refused to come out "just for a cat."

We didn't have a dog, but Robin had a little toy dog he carried everywhere with him. In spite of the fact that you couldn't, ever, make him do anything he did not want to do, Robin was a tender child, and he never let Max, his little brown fluffy dog, out of his sight. Max traveled across continents, to visit Richard's relatives in America, to visit my family in England. He came with us to France, to Rome, and up the Leaning Tower of Pisa. When we finally settled in Pennsylvania, Max accompanied us, and was with Robin when he started kindergarten. He even went to camp when Robin was twelve. When Robin died, in California, he was grown, but Max was still sitting on his bed at home. The other children suggested we take Max to the funeral in California. So Max traveled one last time.

I COULDN'T CARE much about anything, even dogs, when Luggs first came to stay. I only wanted, if possible, to do something for Beth, to whom I owed so much.

Richard had always accepted whatever animals I brought home, and Luggs was greeted kindly by him. Nemo accepted Luggs too, with no caveats except his food bowl, and his kennel. Luggs was inky black and pedi-greed. Nemo was black and brown, and of mixed ances-try, mostly German shepherd.

After Paul had gone, we went on an exploratory walk around the grounds. Boy, was Luggs excited! Nemo ran round him yelping, and Luggs shot off across the lawn, with me ineffectually hanging onto his leash, which was retractable like a fishing line. I fell flat on my face but hung on, and the whirring reel cut a large slice into my hand. He dragged me along and ingested about half a pound of deer scat. Somehow we got back to the house.

The next day, bandaged hand and all, I decided to pick raspberries on the adjacent farm to send back with Luggs as a present. So off we went, the dogs and myself, to pick. Nemo bounded around and chased through the raspberry rows, but Luggs of course was tied, as I had promised. I fixed him to a post at the end of the raspberry row, where he looked longingly after Nemo, and I proceeded to fill my basket. I was at the far end of the row away from him when the farm truck, loaded with pickers, drove up the dirt path toward where he was tied. I rushed out, scream-ing and waving, but the truck drove steadily onward, and when I waved and shouted, the pickers, who didn't speak English, waved merrily and shouted back. Luggs was busy watching Nemo, and the pickers apparently didn't see Luggs at all, but drove right over him, pinning him to the ground by his leash. Finally they stopped. I was hysterical.

Luggs was unhurt. He was lying by the side of the truck, wagging his tail and waiting, and the lead was tangled up under and around the exhaust pipe. Torrents of Spanish; gesticulations; pats on the back; smiles. Someone unclipped the leash and crawled under the truck to free it. Luggs stayed quietly waiting, gently wagging his tail, not attempting now to go anywhere. But he did manage to swallow about a pound of picked raspberries while we were busy untangling him.

Finally we got through that first dog-sitting weekend and I, who told Beth (almost) everything, never confessed how near to disaster we came.

Gradually Luggs and I got to know each other, and we never did have another incident as bad as the one in the raspberry patch. At first, though, I was terrified most of the time—terrified Luggs would get hurt, run away, get sick, perhaps die. But even as we got used to each other I still remained too nervously solicitous about my therapist's dog, never relaxed about him as I was with my own dog. If anything happened to Luggs, I thought, I would never be able to see Beth again. I would be left with no place to rest awhile, safe from the demons that plagued me. I pictured driving past her office, and knowing I couldn't go in. That was to happen, but not because of her dog.

On Guard

B ETH WANTED TO teach me acceptance. Although I was a poor pupil, she would listen quietly while I complained about the government, the church, the environment, my children, God, my mother-in-law, death, bad drivers (not necessarily in that order).

"You know, you can't change everything. You're just going to have to accept what you can't change."

"That's what people say, that's why things don't change."

"Your list of changes is quite long, you know!" She paused. "You can't change God, or death." What did she mean? I became anxious. I had had enough of death.

"Yes you can. People are always redefining their ideas of God and death. That's why we have wars."

"You're not listening. What you can't change, you have to accept." What was she trying to tell me? I didn't want warnings. I wanted her to make everything right, at least in the future. Even if I could be strong, I didn't want to be strong. I wanted *her* to be strong for me.

Although we had lived in Pennsylvania for twenty years before Robin's death, I still felt far from my dearest friends, and my sister, on whose advice I had always depended, was gone. My mother, to whom I had become closer after Anna's death, died too, soon after her eldest daughter. I had crept out of my desolation, seeming to see from the wilderness Beth's friendly warmth, like a comforting fire. Like a puppy, I was drawn toward it.

Indeed, the very first dogs adopted by humans were probably puppies who crept out of the wilderness to the shelter of human campsites or villages, becoming increasingly docile the longer they lived with people. Dogs accept humans. I too had come out of my wilderness into the warmth of Beth's fire, and I wanted her to protect me. But that meant I would have to accept her ideas, of which I was suspicious.

"You're trying to make me into a different person," I grumbled.

"No. No, no. I'd miss you if you were different. I just want to help you. So you can manage your life."

I suppose, in spite of criticizing Beth's theories, I had half-expected a therapist to "straighten me out." I had even nervously thought Beth might reprimand me for my complete inability to endure what was not a unique situation. Every minute of every day people were suffering similarly "unbearable" losses. Other people had lost a child and were presumably walking around, sleeping, and eating. Here was I, I who had once believed I could manage anything, unable to cope, tagging after Beth like a lost, starving puppy. I really wanted her to tell me she would always be there, to laugh kindly at my worries, and tell me they were unfounded. But she did not do this.

When Beth first told me I was "special," I felt really flattered. I don't know how I had missed the universal application of so common a compliment—I suppose by not keeping in touch with the world around me. However, at some later time she mentioned another client who was "special." Jealously, I inquired if many of her clients could be so described. Not only other clients but, it appeared, everybody was "special." Gravely she explained that everyone was a "special person." I bristled.

"Everybody *can't* be special. It's a negation of terms. 'Special' means that you are in some way different from the others."

"Everybody *is* different, in their own special way."

"No, 'special' means singularly different as opposed to everybody else. You're just using the term to try to make everyone feel good. It's psychological jargon."

"I am a psychologist. You're talking like a writer." We glared at each other. It was toward the end of a session and she rose smoothly. She was one of those large women who move with peculiar grace.

"You *are* special," she said kindly. I was not mollified.

"I suppose everybody's special, until proven guilty," I growled. As usual she laughed. Crossly, I thought she used her laugh like a punctuation mark, to bridge awkward moments. When she inquired when we could "get together" next week, I asked grumpily if she really wanted to see me? "If you want to come." Of course I did. I wished it didn't always have to be my decision. Even the dog made it clear he *wanted* to go for a walk with me.

I was becoming attached, by a frail umbilical cord, to a new promise of life, but it also meant this new life depended on Beth. She took it in stride, as I took Luggs's adoration of me in stride.

HER DOG WAS hard to resist, whatever I thought about the evanescence of his affections, for Luggs had a pleasing way of making me feel unique. The moment when I came home was as complete a joy to him as the dawning of a new day after a dark night or, more accurately in his case, the dawning of a new breakfast-time. He threw himself utterly into his delight at my existence, with every particle of his body, nose, tongue, paws, tail. Large, dignified Nemo was clearly pleased to see me too, but without the total abandonment of Luggs. Labrador retrievers like Luggs are the most popular dogs in America, largely because of their effusive friendliness. Luggs would lay his heavy head on my lap and gaze adoringly up at me with soft brown eyes. If I so much as crossed the room, his tail would thump on the floor. It was impossible not to return such love. I knew perfectly well, however, that when Luggs went home he would greet Paul with similar enthusiasm, just as I uneasily knew that when the next client came along, Beth's concern and tenderness would probably be no less than it had been for me. She would "hear" and comfort the next person too.

When Luggs stayed with us, the morning "walkies," as I called our treks, was the high point in the dogs' day. I would go to the closet to get a coat and they would start thumping and circling, whining with excitement. The trouble was, the coat didn't always mean walkies. Sometimes it meant I was going out in the car, or going for a bicycle ride. It depended on the hat, the shoes, and the pocketbook. If I was going out in the car, I would take my pocketbook. I only had to pick it up for them to stop thumping their tails and look at me as if their hearts were broken. Shoes meant biking, but sometimes could also mean a short walk. Rubber boots were ecstasy, almost always meaning mud and fields. Just to hold them was to show the dogs the Holy Grail, and putting boots on caused almost uncontrollable excitement. But occasionally, traitor that I was, rubber boots only meant going to the garden. And so it went, excitement, disappointment, followed by acceptance. They would look crestfallen, and then go back to their rugs. *I* was the one who spent the rest of the morning in guilty discomfort, until finally it could be real walkies, boots and all, with the same prelude of joy.

Beth, though approving of dog walkies, was always urging me to have more to do with the "real" world. She thought I should "go out" more often. She loved to eat out, and sometimes recommended restaurants to me. It was no good telling her that we preferred eating at home. She loved movies, and sometimes enthused about one, seeming disappointed when I didn't respond. Truth was, most movies left me sleepless for nights, their reality, I suppose, being a bit much for someone whose main stimulation came from trudging through muddy fields. One time she announced she had seen a film she knew I "would love," and that wouldn't upset me. "It's about exploration," said she, "and the only death in it is when they have to eat the dogs."

What? I wondered if she knew me as well as I thought. Eat the dogs? We straightened it out, more or less, but I think it was the last time she suggested a movie! We had given up on books quite a while back. I sometimes wonder what happened to the books that I gave her, and that she said she "looked forward" to reading. But, after all, I had refused outright the books *she* had offered me on "loss," or "grieving," etc. I wanted real comfort, not comfort from a book.

ALTHOUGH I RESPECTED and admired Beth, in our relationship *she* was always right, and I sometimes found this frustrating. Even though I argued, her opinions (at least her psychological opinions) didn't budge. She even seemed to expect me to be irritable with her, I suppose as a manifestation of my anger at fate, and I found it even more frustrating when she soothingly talked about "anger" as if it were a curable quality. I wanted her sympathy, unadulterated by opinions on my state of mind, and anyway I didn't think of myself as an angry person, just an unfortunate one.

Anger frightens us, in ourselves or in dogs. And sometimes if we don't feel "special" enough ourselves, we try to get a fierce dog to make up for it. The Romans took fierce Celtic mastiffs, huge guard dogs, back home from Britain to use for baiting animals. In the circus arena, four dogs were considered the right number to bait a lion, three for a bear, and one against an armed man. The fight went on until the dogs, or their opponent, were dead. John Caius, the sixteenth-century author of *De Canibus Britannicus (Of British Dogs)*, said mastiffs were so named from the words "master thief," because they were "the principall causes of their [the thieves] apprehension." More likely the name comes from the Latin *mansuetus* "tame," which in turn comes from *manus,* "hand." Anyone can control a gentle dog, but it's harder to tame a fierce one. To do so can reflect the owner's strength. Some people get a kick out of controlling a potentially lethal dog, as they might out of possessing a lethal weapon. It makes them feel powerful.

Some dogs have a reputation for ferocious anger, although individuals within that breed can be gentle and friendly. Doberman pinschers, which often scare people, were originally developed by Ludwig Dobermann, a German tax collector, reputedly because he needed a dog to protect him from peevish tax evaders. Many people own gentle, friendly Dobermans, and anyway these days tax collectors seem to manage without dogs.

After we met in Italy and before we moved back there, where our three youngest children were born, Richard and I had lived in America for a bit. It was during the Vietnam War, and Richard withheld his taxes in protest. We lived, with our two eldest children, in a tiny wooden house in Vermont, and we had not yet married. After the tax return it wasn't long before a gentleman from the IRS arrived at our house, presumably to seize what property he could, although most of our possessions came from the Salvation Army store. The tax collector arrived at about teatime, a sacred hour for Britishers like myself. Richard was horrified that I offered the tax collector tea, complete with cookies. I tried to explain that teatime, for the British at least, crosses the frontiers of political disagreement. That particular tax collector didn't find anything in our house to collect. He of course had no fierce dog, and we didn't have a dog at the time either. So he left replete with tea and cookies and in the end the IRS froze Richard's art gallery revenue.

German shepherds can be trained to kill, and they look enough like wolves to make most people approach one with caution. Delivery people would never get out of their trucks before they knew our gentle Nemo. We didn't know what his shepherd ancestry was mixed with, but he was large even for a German shepherd.

Nemo had a recognizable moral code regarding ferocity. He was merciless to groundhogs. He chased cats, but never hurt them. He barked at cyclists, but did not chase them. He loved delivery vans and actually tried to get inside the UPS van sometimes, with what intention I do not know.

We kept hens, which scratched and pecked freely around our house. Nemo killed one early on, and we taught him, firmly, that this was not acceptable. After that the hens knew they were perfectly safe, and one matronly mother hen not only shared his food bowl (while he stood anxiously back) but decided to lay a clutch of eggs inside his kennel. Like a gentleman, Nemo vacated the kennel until the eggs hatched and the mother hen marched out, followed by her fragile brood. On the other hand, if geese dared land near our pond, he went for them with terrifying growls. As a very young dog he chased rabbits, squirrels, and deer, too. It was rather sad to see him, as he matured, accept the fact that he would never catch any of these animals, and not even try to chase them. It reminded me of human youth, which chases the swiftest and the highest-flying dreams, but later settles to pursue the slower goals, the groundhogs in our lives.

After his orgies with the unfortunate animals he caught, Nemo was sometimes sick—in which case we left him outside for the night. Not so, as I soon discovered, with Luggs. Once, Beth told me, they had been up all night, because Luggs had ingested a peach stone and had had to be rushed to the vet. After various X rays and explorations he had regurgitated the peach stone. It had cost them a lot of money, she said, but she did not seem to consider there had been an alternative. As usual (although that was certainly not her intention), whenever the subject of money came up, I felt guilty because I wasn't paying her. But I wasn't used to monitoring a dog's digestive problems. What would happen, I wondered, if Luggs got sick when he was staying with us? Even if I thought Luggs was "special," Richard wouldn't take kindly to driving around looking for a vet at midnight because a dog had a stomachache.

Of course, we did take our dogs to the vet if they were really ill, and Richard, who never went to a doctor himself unless he could barely stand, drove miles one Sunday to get Nemo stitched up when he cut his paw and our own vet couldn't be contacted.

Most Americans these days care tenderly for their pets, and emergency centers are open all night—where we live, anyway. It seemed, though, that Luggs was always being rushed to the vet for minor problems. I didn't, of course, tell Beth that I thought this, but I did tell her I had been reading how in the classical world animals could expect little compassion and no rights.

Romans and Greeks kept sheepdogs and guard dogs. An ancient mosaic in Pompeii announced, *Cave canem*, or "beware of the dog," to visitors. The convulsed body of a chained dog, vainly struggling to free itself in the volcanic inferno, was found among the ruins of Pompeii. The Romans used dogs as messengers, too, sometimes making them swallow military orders in a metal tube, and then killing them to retrieve the message at its destination. Even so, a few dog tombs remain from those times, commemorating special dogs. One said, "Do not laugh, I beg you, you passing by, because it is a mere dog's grave." The story of Argus, Odysseus' dog, who faithfully waited for him to return home and then died, still moves us.

Like the guard dog in Pompeii, dogs signal a warning by barking. The puppies of both wolves and dogs have similar yelping barks, which they use to attract attention, but adult wolves, although so closely related to dogs, hardly ever bark, and never bark at length like dogs. We presume barking was encouraged and selected by humans early on in our partnership with dogs. Early explorers of the New World, however, reported that the dogs kept by American Indians did not bark.

The verb *bark* has Anglo-Saxon and Icelandic roots. The bark of dogs has nothing to do with the bark of trees, except perhaps when a dog "barks up the wrong tree" (an old hunting expression). Tree "bark" comes from an Icelandic word, *börker*, meaning "stem," and the Middle English word *barke* ("rind"). The dog's "bark" comes from the Anglo-Saxon *bearcan*, "to bluster," which is what dogs are often doing, especially when their "bark is worse than their bite." Dogs, as any mailman will attest, can also bite, but usually a silent dog is more apt to bite than a noisy barker. Barking doesn't necessarily mean anger, but growling with ears laid back is definitely a hostile signal.

Sometimes I felt that I, too, frantically barked, endeavoring to attract Beth's attention and affection. It was not until much later that I realized her allowing me to care for Luggs was no ordinary gesture for a therapist. Perhaps Beth had even been allowing me to participate in her private life as part of my therapy, unconventional though it was. I clung to Beth's strength most of the time, even when I wasn't with her. In my dimmed world there seemed little else to look forward to other than the weekly visits to her office. Were others feeling the same when she was with them? When Luggs was with me, he entered completely into my world. I was "the one" for him. Did Beth seem to others as totally part of *their* world as when she was with me? Did she, like Luggs, forget about me in the interval between visits? Occasionally Beth would mention that she had "thought of me" when she had read a certain book or when Britain had been in the news. It was something, but I needed a mother who thought of me all the time, a sister who had shared my whole past life, a son who was in my unconscious night and day. Even those who remained, and whom I still loved, seemed to have grown very distant from me, to be waving at me sadly from the other side of some transparent wall of sorrow dividing us.

Different Species

A S A VERY YOUNG child, during World War II, I lived in what was then the British Mandate of Palestine. The barbed wire around the compound where we lived, the adults' grim faces around the radio with its gold-meshed front, were intimations of a dangerous world for all who lived there, Jews, Arabs, and British. Our dog, Susie, was one of those mop-like dogs of no known parentage. We children (there were three of us then) amused ourselves most of the time, since our parents were always busy and worried by war. Susie was an important adjunct to our lives, and I vividly remember when she bit my elder sister, Anna, who was a more stable part of my life than even my mother. Susie was supposed to be the "audience" for a play we were staging. But she was sitting with her bone, in the wrong place to see the show, and when Anna tried to move the bone, Susie changed from a soft mop of hair to an indignant snapping of sharp white teeth. So can life change instantly from bright warmth to snapping danger.

Beth, whom I liked to think of as an older sister and whose professional role I was choosing to ignore, suggested that my present losses might be even harder to accept because of an unstable childhood. Although I welcomed her comfort, I could not agree. The pain I felt now could imagine no alternative background that could have lessened it. My grief was nearer to that of a wounded dog than of a person.

Certainly, however, sudden death was introduced to me early. I can still see the radio 'round which we huddled, listening to the names of my parents' friends who were killed when the Jewish Stern Gang, in opposition to the British, blew up the King David hotel. The world was unsafe, and I was afraid.

I knew that Beth was trying to help me, so, because she was interested, I told her about my early life. We were still in Palestine when both my parents were hospitalized with tuberculosis, and my elder brother and sister were sent back to boarding school in Britain. I was under the care of a very young, new, Arab nurse. My former Jewish nurse, whom I had loved from babyhood, had been left behind when we moved from Jerusalem to Jaffa. In Jaffa we were guarded by British soldiers, with whom my nurse flirted deliciously, and who made a pet of me. They used to let me into their sand bunker to play with their machine guns, which had handles that twirled around like giant rattles. They gave me chewing gum, and I spent hours in the bunkers, playing and chattering with them. I suppose they were lonely. They treated me like a little princess, honoring my every wish.

Wild tortoises were abundant, and some children kept them as pets. Sometimes the boys drilled a tiny hole in the corner of the shell so their tortoises could wander on a long string. Our dog, Susie, had disappeared from our lives, and I longed for a pet. My parents had kept rabbits, but these I found were dangerous to love, because they were raised for meat. I still remember discovering *after* lunch that I had eaten an adorable black-and-white rabbit we called Whiskey.

I wanted a pet tortoise. When I told my soldier friends, they promised me one. Duly, when I came to the bunker, there was an exceptionally large tortoise waiting for me. We crouched around it in the damp, sandbagged hole, watching it slowly stick its head out of the shell and hiss. I took that as a signal that it liked me.

My soldier friends were anxious that I should enjoy my present, and had even shined its shell for me with gun oil. They were so eager to please me, those young British soldier boys, far from home. When I asked for a small hole in the corner of its shell, so that it should not escape, they nodded enthusiastically, and one of them produced a hammer and a nail. As I have said, they were young and far from home, and I think they were probably as terrified as I when the blow from the nail exploded the beautiful domed shell apart, and blood spurted all over the damp sand. I seem to remember them calling me back in cracked, anxious voices when I left the bunker running, running from the shattering stupidity of war, and the disasters of ignorance.

IT ISN'T SURPRISING that we agonize over miscommunication with animals, because even with language as a tool, we so often can't connect with one another. When I began seeing Beth, I had lived much of my life in other countries and cultures, and our friends were mostly artists. I had had little contact with the popular media, and had never had any interest in psychology. "Transference," "pushing the right buttons," "I hear you," "your space," "owing to yourself," "what you deserve" were a few of the phrases new to me. Yes, I had argued about her use of "special," but in fact I was rather awed by the aptness of some terms, thinking that they were her own expressions, and admiring her cleverness. It was not until later that I realized such expressions were professional, and in general use.

However, when Beth told me I was her "client," not her "patient," I again responded as a writer. I went to the dictionary to clarify the two words. A "patient," it seemed, might be ill, perhaps also willing to wait patiently for the doctor. A "client" was seeking the "services of a professional." Was I "seeking her services"?

Some might wonder why I didn't do a little more research into her professional reasons for calling me a "client" and her other points of view that puzzled me. I was, after all, used to research, and I could have read psychological theory, or even asked her what to expect. I think it was because very soon I sought not her profession but her comfort. Even if at first I had expected some kind of professional service, soon I simply wanted someone to fill the terrible void left by those whom I had lost. Anyway, I dutifully became a "client," even though I didn't much like it, particularly when she referred to other (anonymous, of course) "clients" and their problems, some of which were similar to mine.

Even so, the British-educated snob writer in me couldn't help judging these new terms. As I grew to know Beth better, I felt more confident about telling her my opinions. Unmoved, she continued to call me her "client," and give psychological titles to my feelings. She was beginning to try to teach me paths through my desolation. Although I argued with her terminology, I respected her absolute certainty in her ability to help me. In a way that's how we train dogs, too. They succumb to the certainty that ours is the better way. If we are inconsistent or uncertain, we can't succeed in training them.

I was technically going to Beth for "grief counseling," but many of my visits were not glum. She loved to hear the bizarre stories about my life, of which there always seemed to be a good supply. In Pennsylvania, we lived with my mother-in-law for almost twenty-five years, and her sister, also an erstwhile southern belle, lived a few miles away. The new language and terrain of counseling might have been strange, but it was nothing compared to the mysteries of my in-laws' world. I could learn the new rules of Beth's profession, but my American relations made the rules as they went along.

This was grist for a psychologist's mill. How firmly and gravely Beth would tell me about "my space," and what everybody in our family "owed" each other. I always wished she could have been right there, when my mother-in-law walked into our closed bedroom, seeming not to worry whether Richard and I were in bed together, to ask me if her shoes matched her dress. On another occasion Richard's aunt fainted and had to be revived when we said we might have to spend Thanksgiving elsewhere and could not have a family dinner. Beth assumed that if I "made myself clear," the two old ladies would understand and of course comply. Maybe I just didn't do it right. They always seemed to end up in bed (nursed by me) whenever I tried Beth's way.

That didn't stop Beth rolling with laughter when I recounted being called out of the shower at the town swimming pool (by the police) to rescue the old dears when they had landed in the Emergency Room after a particularly good lunch out. Both the sisters had fainted on the way out of the restaurant that time, but the doctors hadn't been trained by Beth either, and had tested their vital signs, rather than asking them if they had enjoyed cocktails for lunch. They were both in their nineties. When I arrived at the hospital, an admiring young doctor was in the middle of telling Richard's aunt how "wonderful" she looked for her age. I mentioned the cocktails. Unsurprisingly, in retrospect, she grumbled that I had "spoilt everything."

I mustn't, said Beth, when she had finished laughing, let myself be "manipulated." Quite right. But what are you to do with the people you love? What are you to do, after all, with a dog like Luggs, who eats peach pits and keeps you up all night with the consequences?

However successfully Beth guided people, her dog, from my point of view, was not well trained. If I let Luggs loose, he didn't come when called, returning only when he pleased. He loved the snow, especially when it was deep and I went skiing in the fields around us, because then I couldn't keep him on a leash. He'd tear 'round in circles or dash in front of my skiis, often stopping to burrow under the snow for (of course) something to eat. One Christmas vacation, Luggs was with us, and it snowed heavily. Chuck, our second-youngest son, and I went out on skiis, taking the dogs along. Luggs disappeared. We called and searched, our whistles echoing ineffectively from the silent snowy woods, but we couldn't even find pawprints. Finally we went home. Luggs had arrived before us. He had appeared with a mouthful of deer entrails (left by a hunter) dripping onto the snow. It was impossible to imagine a happier being, said Richard, than Luggs standing blackly, tail wagging wildly and blood dripping from his mouth onto the gleaming snow. However, we left it to *him* to tell Paul of his adventure.

When scolded, Beth's dog simply wagged his tail. When Luggs "stole" food, Beth told me, his criminal menu included the most unlikely things. Once, Beth said, he ate a whole pound of coffee beans, with disastrous results. Another time, he ate a complete box of hemorrhoidal suppositories, which had, surprisingly, glided right through him, tinfoil casing and all. I didn't like to ask their intended destination. I knew her better by then, but not that well!

Beth didn't seem to think there was much you could do about Luggs, even though she clearly believed that her job included training her clients to redirect their thoughts, and so their lives. She certainly seemed to have taken on training *me* with confidence.

We might have been two different species. I didn't believe I could do much to influence my own destiny, but I still believed that with enough patience you could train dogs. I had spent hours, days, training our Nemo, until he fit well into the family. We were used to putting food on the counter, confident it would not be touched. We could leave him free all day, expecting him to wait at home for us to return. The only time we could do little with him was when the weather was stormy. He would cower in the shower stall, although he knew we didn't encourage this, because he left hairs in the drain. But, along with many

34

churches, I accepted that morality includes a few minor lapses, and anyway I am afraid of thunder myself. Although I scolded Luggs for taking food, I was too uneasy about just how to instill a sense of honesty, much less guilt, in a psychologist's dog! Consequently, when he stayed with us, we never could leave him alone in the kitchen.

Beth practiced what she called "cognitive therapy." Her idea, as I understood it, was that by standing back and looking at one's behavior, or emotions, one would more easily be in control to make rational "choices" and direct one's thoughts "positively." Although she wanted to help me, and I wanted to be helped, we still had problems connecting. Just because I knew *why* I was unhappy, angry, and so on, why would that make it better for me? "Call it what you like," I would obstinately growl at her, like a dog with a sore paw, "giving things names doesn't make any difference. You can't change things happening. You can't stop people hurting. Or loving. Or dying."

"That's not what we're trying to do," she would say, and then tell me to "have a good week." I knew I wasn't going to change her ideas (and I'm not sure I even really wanted to). Perhaps I feared that her theories might make me a case, a problem, rather than a person. Perhaps I didn't *want* my thoughts trained along new paths, even if it might make life easier.

Whenever I protested that I "didn't believe" in psychology, Beth good-naturedly pointed out that I kept on coming. I told her that it was she, not her profession, that drew me. She replied that she could not separate herself from her profession. Stubbornly, however, I just wanted to be loved. I tried, though, to take her advice when she gave it, and I did learn the new words.

To survive, dogs have had to please us, and their aim in life is still to please. Even dogs that attack humans have usually been trained to do so by other humans, for, with rare exceptions, dogs want to love humans, whether or not humans are lovable. One theory is that dogs consider humans as a sort of "alpha dog," so they instinctively submit to them. Some trainers recommend treating your dog as if you were an alpha dog or wolf, because an aggressive dog is one that in reality is too fearful and insecure, needing to be reassured by knowing its place in the pack. Others feel that dogs best respond to kindness under all circumstances. Anyway, Beth was certainly an alpha dog as far as I was concerned.

Just as a puppy will be trained because of its love for the trainer, not for the sake of the training goal, and still protesting that "taking pills" was no solution to losing those I had loved, I even agreed to try taking antidepressants for a while. I said I would do so to please her. She replied that it didn't matter what my reasons were as long as I took them. I didn't know if they actually helped or not. But I did know that without the weekly visit to her office, I would have been lost.

A Black Dog on One's Back

A s I GOT TO know Luggs better, Beth got to know more about me. We went on exploring my early childhood.

My father was unable to work and we left Palestine. Tuberculosis, in the days before antibiotics, was considered a fatal disease, and the only known cure was complete rest in clear mountain air. So my mother and father were sent to a sanatorium in Switzerland, and we children were farmed out to various relatives in Britain. We were not told that our parents would recover, because it was probably thought unlikely that they would. I was sent to live in Scotland with my paternal grandparents.

My years in Scotland were often gray and melancholy. After Robin died, everything was without color. When I first started going to Beth, my world was often similar in substance and color to a black-and-white movie.

Depressed people, like dogs, sometimes don't see colors well. Most people think that dogs see only grays, or black and white. In fact, although they don't see our full color spectrum, they do see some color. Apparently they are unable to tell red from yellow and green, or violet from blue. They see better in the dark than we do.

Dogs get to know each other, and us, largely by smell. The diverse tints of their coats have been imposed on them by us. In ancient times sheepdogs were bred from white mutants, so they would blend with the sheep (and fool predators), and also be distinguishable to the shepherd from dark wolves. Sometimes their ears were encouraged to be floppy, so they would look as unlike wolves as possible. Guard dogs were dark, often with pricked ears, like threatening wild animals.

Luggs was black all over, except for his brown eyes. I thought he was beautiful, naturally. I was prejudiced before I even saw him. Beth had not told me what *color* her dog was. It would never have occurred to her, because most of us don't think of an actual black dog signifying anything. Luggs himself, an effusive companion from dawn to dusk, wetly licking me whenever he got a chance, was anything but depressing.

"Having a black dog on your back" signifies depression. Those who suffer depression often describe it as seeming like an actual physical weight, which perceptibly lifts when things improve. Sometimes it's a large black bird rather than a black dog.

In our culture, other colors have different associations. Shimmying pink elephants are seen by those who have drunk too much, and red is everywhere at Christmas, while Easter is pale green and mauve. But although color symbols vary within cultures, black mostly signifies darkness, and white, light: "But I am black, / as if bereav'd of light," wrote William Blake. Black can also represent power and formality, as in judicial robes, or men's evening wear. The Fascist Black Shirts were dressed to inspire fear. Hamlet described the "customary suits of solemn black . . . the suits of woe."

In the past, people have had a complicated relationship with black dogs. They have been thought of as a somber symbol in our lives. Spartan youths, looking for strength in battle, sacrificed black puppies to Ares, the god of war. Hecate, goddess of the underworld, also had black dogs sacrificed to her, and sometimes a black dog was killed and buried at a crossroads, in the hopes of making journeys safer for travelers. At night Hecate haunted tombs and crossroads, accompanied by her retinue of demon dogs, unseen by humans but barked at by earthly dogs.

Clerics often wore black, but the Dominican monks wore a white lining under their black hooded cloaks, to represent the purity of white and new life, as well as the blackness of mortification and death. The Dominican order was also connected with dogs. St. Dominic's mother, Joan de Guzman or Joan of Aza, had prayed for a son. She dreamed her prayer was answered, although in the dream she gave birth to a dog, which ran out into the world carrying a flaming torch in its mouth. When her son was born she called him Dominic, and he grew up to found the Dominican order, a name that (mindful of the dream) can be translated as *Domini canes* or, in Latin, "the hounds of God." The dog is a Dominican symbol, and St. Dominic was believed to have the power to cure rabies. Dalmatian lovers sometimes claim that the original dream dog was a black-and-white Dalmatian, as in the colors of the Dominican robes.

Women could once be condemned as witches for having too close a friendship with black dogs, which were associated with the devil, though not as important to witchcraft as black cats. In Goethe's *Faust,* a jet black poodle circles ever closer around Faust and Wagner as they walk through the cornfields at dusk. Wagner says it is lost and looking for its master. He points out that the dog sits, growls, and wags its tail, "all canine orthodox." So Faust is persuaded to ignore the "little tongues of fire" around the running dog, which follows him home, duly turns into a phantom with "fearful fangs and fiery, staring brow," and is really Mephistopheles' hound from hell.

Another legendary black dog was, in real life, white. Prince Rupert, who fought for Charles I in the British Civil War, had a large white poodle named Boy, from whom he was inseparable. For a while every battle that Rupert fought, accompanied by Boy, was victorious, and the dog was known by the Puritans as "more than halfe a divell . . . whelped in Lap-land where . . . none but divells and sorcerers live." They thought that Boy could make himself invisible, speak several languages, and be invulnerable in battle. Neither prayers nor poison administered by the Roundheads seemed to have any effect, until finally, in 1644, Boy was killed at the Battle of Marston Moor. Coincidentally (or not?), the tide of the war thereafter turned in favor of Cromwell's army. The Puritans circulated a pamphlet celebrating Boy's death, gleefully stating that "Close mourners are the witch, Pope and Devill." But although the real dog was white, in the pamphlet he is shown as *black*. By 1717, the Duchess of Orleans described her uncle Rupert's dog as "a great black dog, which was his companion, [and] was the devil." White dogs were considered beautiful and unthreatening, and black dogs were not popular pets.

If ancient beliefs still applied, black would certainly be

the wrong color for a therapist's dog, especially if, like Beth, she was working to relieve my depression, rather than lending me a black symbol of it.

Luggs did cheer me, but Beth seemed to think, regardless of circumstances, I might tend toward depression, and it is true that I remembered times of melancholy before. Scotland, after Palestine, was a grim, dark place. How strange it was, after the relentless heat seeping into everything, after the brilliant light and the metallic pitch of Arabic voices, to be shrouded in dim mist. Even the conversations seemed dulled. I found it hard to understand the blurred talk, and kept half-hearing anxious whispering, which I suspected was about me or my parents.

I was eventually told that if I behaved very well, my mother or father *might* get better. Fairies, said the cook, were on the lookout to make sure that I did behave. After this injunction, I was pretty much left on my own. I missed the vibrant excitement of Palestine, even the throbbing sense of danger. My Arabic nurse, with her flaming red hair, had been emotional and short-tempered, kissing or slapping me unpredictably, but there was never a feeling of secrecy about her, as there was with my grandmother's cook, who was now in charge of me. I called her Mrs. Patterson, but although she had a sleepy teenage daughter, Mr. Patterson, if he had ever existed, was never mentioned.

My grandmother took little notice of me, but my grandfather jigged me on his knee sometimes, and told me stories. However, a short time after I arrived, they both went on a trip, leaving me with Mrs. Patterson (and the fairies). Then, suddenly, there were even more whispers behind my back, more covert glances in my direction. Uneasy I tried to catch what it was all about. At night, awake in my brass bed in the second maid's room (where I slept to be near Mrs. Patterson), I wondered sadly if my mother had died. After several anxious days, I was lying on the hearth rug of the cook's sitting room, poking at the dingy pink roses on a tufty black background. Mrs. Patterson came in and sat in the chair next to the fire.

"Don't do that," she said, "you're pulling that rug to pieces." She paused. "I might as well tell you. Your grandfather died. Leave that rug alone, would you? There won't be anything left of it if you go on like that."

That evening she came to turn out the light. The room was chillingly cold, but I had a stone hot water bottle to warm the bed. It had a screw top, which was always slightly hotter than the bottle itself. By morning it was like a cold, clammy rock by my feet, but at bedtime it was scorching hot.

Grandfather, said Mrs. Patterson, was now in Heaven, where, *if* I was good, I would see him in due course. Her duty done, she abruptly snapped out the light. I lay there. If I maneuvered the bottle to just the right place, I could keep a bit warmer, but it was still a hard, uncomforting lump. I cried, but more for my mother, I think, than for my grandfather. Anyway, I certainly wanted to go to Heaven, whether he was there or not. I had just been told in the Presbyterian Sunday school about the fiery pits of Hell, so I would have to be very good indeed. This was harder under Mrs. Patterson than it had been when I lived with my mother, whom I remembered, although ever less clearly, as a laughing lady who usually dressed in green.

In my grandmother's huge, misty garden, I took care to avoid woody areas where most likely the fairies lurked, and I sought what companionship I could. Not much comfort could be found in the dog, a bad-tempered, elderly Dandie Dinmont terrier, who would have nothing to do with a lonely little girl. My grandfather had been an ardent admirer of all things Scottish, but especially the novels of Sir Walter Scott. Dandie Dinmonts are border terriers named after a character in the Scott novel *Guy Mannering*, and were bred to hunt otters and badgers. The original terriers in "Dandie's pack" were described by Scott as chasing a tax collector "on his ominous rounds." Like many terriers, they can be less beguiling than they look. Robey, as my grandmother's dog was called, kept me well clear of him. He looked adorable, with silky gray fur. But sharp little teeth emerged from that hirsute charm whenever I approached him. Mrs. Patterson loved him, calling him in a high, wheedling voice, which I soon learned to distinguish from the voice she used to summon me.

I fixed my attention on the large tortoise that lived on the walled terrace. I would probably have preferred something more cuddly, but once again, it seemed the most available creature I might love. After all, I had learned to find warmth in a stone hot-water bottle! Was I also trying to replace that disastrous tortoise in Palestine?

Anyway, I crouched daily on my grandmother's damp terrace and fed this tortoise dandelion leaves. It ate happily from my hand, but who knows to what extent such a creature could reciprocate my affectionate overtures? Did my new pet mistily perceive a being connected to the proffered dandelions, as I crouched for hours feeding it, sustained by my belief in its fondness for me? Gilbert White, the famous eighteenth-century naturalist, wrote about Timothy, a tortoise whom he adopted after its first owner died. He wondered why "[p]rovidence should bestow such a profusion of days, such a seeming waste of longevity, on a reptile that appears to relish it so little as to squander more than two thirds of its existence in a joyless stupor, and be lost to all sensation for months together in the profoundest of slumbers." Dogs live much shorter lives than tortoises, but love us a lot more. Hard, stone hot-water bottles outlast soft rubber ones.

Puppy Love

YOU CAN'T POSSIBLY be as perfect as I think you are," I remarked to Beth on one visit. She laughed, and told me this was called "transference," which was part of the "healing process." I knew I was not thinking clearly, but surely I had some judgment left. Was love a form of sickness?

Once he got to know me, Luggs was happy to wait at the foot of the stairs all morning until, O joy, I was ready to take him for a walk. Following me around the house, sitting where I sat, walking where I walked. So was I with Beth. At first I counted the hours between my visits, later I improved a little, and only counted the days.

As any dog could tell you, the negative side of love is fear of losing it. If Beth was late for an appointment, I waited in agony, convinced she had been run over, or had decided not to see me, or had eloped to China, or any other lurid disaster that might take her out of my life forever. Ready for tragedy to pounce once more, I never thought she simply might have been held up. I would wait in the parking lot outside her office, despair rolling over me in dense, foggy waves. At first she was casual about not being punctual, but later when she knew what it did to me, she was kind, and always tried to warn me. Even so, I hated that parking lot. Once I waited in the pouring rain. Between the puddles were hundreds of stranded worms. It was a fairly new tarmac lot that had once been a field, and perhaps the worms were trying to reach another desolate oasis of pachysandra on the other side. As I waited, growing more panicky every moment, cars swept in, squashing worms by the dozen under their tires. It became unbearable, and in desperation I started collecting worms in an old paper coffee cup. Squatting across the puddles, soaked through, trying to cram worms into the cup, it seemed as if the world was surely ending. A man in a dark suit, jovial as the devil, asked from under his umbrella if I was "going fishing." Finally Beth came.

This time she gave me paper towels to dry myself, and listened as I hurled abuse at a universe that could let worms be squashed in car parks. She seemed more concerned that I was wet through than that the worms were continuing to be squelched under the wheels of every car that arrived. "Look," I shouted, "you own this building, you can organize everyone in it to collect worms. If everyone collects a hundred worms it won't take long." She nodded seriously, and said she would "see to it later." I knew she lied, but was not going to admit that she was imperfect enough to do so. We talked of other things: She was good at steering my attention from disasters. My own worms I took home and emptied into the compost pile. I continued to believe that Beth was perfect, and to know that she had not saved a single worm (except me).

I suppose from a psychologist's point of view it must be nice, if a little wearisome, to be so admired. Beth explained to me patiently that she was far from perfect, and that such approbation was misplaced. I disagreed, begging her never to retire or move away, and she said that was not her intention. I added that she must never, ever die, because I couldn't take it. She laughed, and said she had no intention of dying either, and she enjoyed life, thank you very much. I worried that I had gone too far.

ONLY HUMANS WORRY about what's appropriate. Dogs have no worries about overdoing their love, and

this is why many people find them irresistible, though nonlovers of dogs might feel the opposite:

"I am your spaniel; and, Demetrius," whines Helen in *A Midsummer Night's Dream,*

> The more you beat me, I will fawn on you.
> Use me but as your spaniel, spurn me, strike me,
> Neglect me, lose me; only give me leave,
> Unworthy as I am, to follow you.

This kind of love in humans might well be considered "co-dependent," transference or not, but dogs have depended on it for their survival. Humans tolerate them, or fall for them, precisely because they accept us on almost any terms.

In Emily Brontë's *Wuthering Heights,* Heathcliff loves his cousin Cathy, who marries Edgar Linton instead of him. So, in revenge, Heathcliff elopes with Edgar's sister, Isabella. Before they leave, Heathcliff, in a vicious departing gesture, hangs Isabella's little spaniel, Fanny, from a bridle hook on the wall. When Isabella pleads for its life, Heathcliff says he wishes he "had the hanging of every being belonging to her." The spaniel is barely saved by the housekeeper, but still tries to run after Isabella. In spite of Heathcliff's unkindness, Isabella herself, spaniel-like, follows him.

Brontë clearly did not like little spaniels, which she describes as "a heap of warm hair." Her own dog, Keeper, was a ferocious mastiff-like mongrel. Once Emily punished him by beating him until his eyes and head swelled. Keeper, however, was devoted to his mistress, and after she died he moaned for nights at the door of her empty room.

"Shall I compare thee to a dogge," as did Sir John Davies in his sixteenth-century poem "In Cineam"? Beth simply, silently, wiped up the mess of my grief, as one cleans up after a quivering puppy. The tissues she handed me were more than practical, they were metaphorical, a symbol for a life spilled uncontrollably at her feet.

Beth's life appeared to me, in comparison to my crumbled world, ordered and brilliant, steered competently by herself. At this point in my therapy I was ready to accept that anything I did or had done could be rethought, and maybe that would somehow remake me. She, I thought, would have been able to cope with what had felled me. But what had felled me would surely not have happened to her. She, I believed, would have been able to have saved my darling Robin, while I had failed. It seemed that everything I had done or believed had been wrong. If I had been more like her, perhaps our lives could have been as blessed as hers seemed to be.

At first she was a comforter, a listener. Any arrogance, any judgment I had once associated with her profession was just not there. Others had told me I would "get over" Robin's death, and I "still had much to be thankful for," or that they too had suffered. I felt guilty for my weakness, and I could not hear them. Yes, I had Richard. We had five sons left, and I still had two brothers. But I had only one heart to be broken.

How lucky I was that my counselor wasn't the great Sigmund Freud. In 1927 he wrote to a friend that his dog Wolf "has almost replaced the lost Heinerle," his four-year-old grandson, who had died. Wolf was, it is true, a remarkable dog. Once, he was lost in Vienna when he had been out walking with Freud's daughter, Anna. Anna could not find Wolf—and it turned out that the dog had jumped into a taxi, exposing his name tag to the cab driver, who brought him home.

After Wolf died he was replaced by a chow, given to Freud by his friend Marie Bonaparte, also a psychoanalyst. She wrote of her dog Topsy (also a chow): "There is nothing of you of those mixed attitudes which are human, in which one loves and hates at the same time. . . . You don't talk, Topsy, nor do you trouble my contemplation by the recital of your woes."

Freud said that "dogs love their friends and bite their

enemies, quite unlike people, who are incapable of pure love." It's ironic that both these pioneers of psychology appear to have found it easier to get along with dogs than with humans. Did they sigh with relief when their patients left the office?

As Beth said, no one "replaces" any being who has died, dog or person. I do not think that I could have been much comforted by a man like Freud, however great. Or however much he loved his dog.

Exposing your life to anyone leaves it open to judgment, which we fear. I was not used to exposing my emotions as I was now learning to do with Beth. In a British family like mine, it was proper to be cheerful at all times, and in dire crisis, we proffered cups of tea. Exposed emotion was, as my young brother once said, "hot-making," and we avoided it.

Beth, of course, *wanted* me to show my emotions. She didn't seem to mind if they included criticism or affection for her, but gravely examined them like a doctor examining one's private parts. But people tend to avoid being naked.

Shortly before he died, Robin told us a story of how he decided to swim in a small lake in New England, and took off his clothes, leaving them on the bank. He reached the opposite shore of the lake and realized with horror that he was too tired to swim back again. So, naked as he was, he had to run around the lake on a path through the woods to get back to his clothes. It was a state park but, luckily, not crowded. He was exceptionally tall and we laughed at the thought of his huge naked form loping through the trees.

We laughed then, but later we cried when we understood how he had hidden his naked emotions from us, so we had not been able to help him. If only he had confided in us. Did he fear that we would think his problems were a weakness, and that we might judge him instead of just helping?

DOGS ALWAYS LOVE, even where humans need to judge. They can, and do, love the strangest people. Hitler's dog Blondi, an Alsatian bitch, was his sole and devoted companion in a bunker at Werewolf. Hitler played with her every evening and taught her to climb a ladder and beg at the top. He evidently adored her, and she responded. Blondi came to the Führer's fifty-fourth birthday party and "sang" with her master. When Hitler's generals conspired against him, he turned to his dog: "Look me in the eyes, Blondi. Are you also a traitor, like the generals of my staff?" Stasi and Negus, Eva Braun's two Scottish terriers, did not, however, accept Blondi, who had to stay away from them, and so from her loving master too, when *his* mistress was around. But Blondi still loved Hitler, and died with him, too, in his bunker, where a vial of cyanide was forced down her throat, just before Hitler and Eva committed suicide.

Another tyrant, Napoléon Bonaparte, was not a dog lover, and was actually bitten by one of his wife's beloved pugs in the midst of conjugal delight on their wedding night. Rather understandably, Napoléon refused to let Josephine's dogs onto the matrimonial bed thereafter, and they had to sleep in an adjacent room, at least when he was around. Even so, in his last years, Napoléon did give tribute to a dog. He was recalling the aftermath of the Battle of Bassano. Walking among the fallen soldiers, Napoléon noticed a dog running out from beside its master's body, and then returning again and again, licking the dead soldier's face and howling mournfully. Finally defeated and exiled, Napoléon recalled his feelings: "Without emotion, I had ordered battles that would decide an army's fate. I had watched the outcome of operations that would sacrifice many men's lives and had not shed a tear. And suddenly I completely lost my composure because of the pitiful howling of a dog."

I too ran back to the remembered faces of my dead, again and again, howling in frantic pain. Beth, veteran of emotional battlefields galore, looked on, saying little, wordlessly hugging me when the appointed hour was over, and it was time to leave. This time luck was on my side. Transference or not, I had landed with someone kind as a mother dog with her little pup.

Dogs and Gods

ACCORDING TO HERODOTUS, when a dog died in ancient Egypt, the family shaved their heads and bodies in mourning. (Cat lovers may think it odd that when a cat died the mourners shaved only their eyebrows.) In ancient Egypt the great and noble expected to continue their lives in another world. The pharaohs' favorite hunting dogs were embalmed, mummified, and put in their tombs with them to hunt in the afterlife. Some of their elaborate jeweled dog collars have survived.

If dogs themselves have doubts, they can't easily convey them to us, so we intrepret their religion as one of waggy acceptance, and we find them very cheering. It's nothing new. The eighteenth-century poet John Wolcot, who used the pseudonym Peter Pindar, wrote an epitaph for his spaniel expressing just such feelings:

Fond of his ease and to no parties prone,
He damned no sect, but calmly gnawed his bone;
Performed his functions well in every way
Blush, Christians, if you can, and copy Tray.

Truly, if we copied Tray we would be happier. Only sectarians would suffer.

BETH ONCE ARRIVED at a session in a rather short purple skirt and high-heeled pumps. She was plump at the time but had very neat legs and ankles.

"Ooh," I had said, "that's a fancy skirt. Who are you trying to impress?"

"No one," said she, primly, crossing her legs and looking a little sheepish. "I'm going to a church council meeting. The bishop will be there."

Of course after that I hadn't been able to resist asking about "the bishop" any time she had arrived dressed up. Beth sang in her church choir. At some point I discovered that her favorite hymn was "Jesus loves me, this I know, / For the Bible tells me so." Try as I would, and admiring Beth as I did, I could not think as she did.

Nor could I achieve what we picture as the lovely simplicity of a dog, a philosophy of life to which even cynics can aspire. The word *cynic* comes from the Greek *kuon,* "dog," because Diogenes, the original Greek cynic, said that unless we think like dogs, happiness will elude us. He is reputed to have made his home in a barrel, really a kind of dog kennel. But although he called himself a dog, Diogenes' desire to be like one was frustrating. He spent his days carrying around a lighted lantern in a human but fruitless search for a moral man!

In spite of my yearnings for assurance, neither Diogenes nor churches like Beth's seemed to meet my own human needs.

Richard was descended from generations of Quakers, and his mother always attended Quaker Meeting. When the children were small we used to take them. They had to sit still and perfectly quiet for twenty minutes and then, as they grew older, for a whole hour. They had ways of passing the hour, no doubt, but it was amazing that a whole roomful of Quaker children could actually sit quietly for that length of time. They could, of course, give the rest of Meeting a "message" if the spirit moved them, but children rarely did this. It was not, however, without some effect. One day little Robin told me solemnly that he liked to climb to the top of a tree and "have Meeting by myself."

I HAD NO DOCTRINAL convictions myself and joined our Quaker Meeting; in fact, Quakers have no formal doctrines, but most religious groups are explicit about things such as eternal life and human souls. The early Christian church decreed firmly that dogs did not have souls. In the thirteenth century, the Dominican theologian Thomas Aquinas wrote, "the life of animals and plants is preserved not for themselves but for man."

Not everyone agreed. Robert Southey, a "lake poet" and a contemporary of Wordsworth, wrote an elegy to his dog Phillis. In it he hopefully proposed that there was an afterlife for dogs, although perhaps not in the same location as the human one: "There is another world / For all that live and more—a better one!" where "proud bipeds . . . may envy thee."

In 1794 David Hartley wrote, "If there be any glimmering of the Hope of an Hereafter for them [animals], this would have a particular Tendency to increase our Tenderness for them." Even the Methodist preacher John Wesley, who denied that God had "equal regard" for animals as for humans, said in a sermon that "one day [animals] shall then receive ample amends for all their present suffering."

Whether or not they believed in an afterlife for animals, plenty of church members loved them. For some members of the church who had relinquished earthly attachments, dogs were a comfort. A thirteenth-century convent firmly ruled that "You shall not possess any beast, my dear sisters, except only a cat." The fourteenth-century archdeacon of Ely, Hugo de Seton, forbade nuns to keep pet dogs, which often lay "beneath the chair, especially during divine service." Services were extremely long and in unheated churches. A cuddly dog to amuse and warm the worshippers was understandably popular. Some churches had to pay "dog whippers" to remove dogs from church.

In the nineteenth century, Darwin's suggestion that we were all descended from apes shook theological foundations. Even a hint of animality in humans bothered the Christian church. A group of ninth-century missionaries had worried whether if, on their voyage to "the end of the earth" (northern Scandinavia), they encountered men with heads like dogs, they should try to convert them. In spite of their dog heads, would these creatures be men if, like ourselves, they covered their genitals? And should they then be saved?

Beth would have been the first to say that she loved people more than she loved dogs. I knew that within her church she was a liberal, supporting controversial rights such as women priests and same-sex marriages.

The rights of all humans were dear to her. But animals? I did not ask her what she considered Luggs's chances for eternal life.

Whatever Beth believed, she was always rather formal, and not only about her religion. She always seemed pleased enough to see Luggs when I brought him back, but there was no rolling around on the grass getting her face licked. Metaphorically, she was always pleased to see me too, but I wasn't going to get a face-licking, grass-rolling reception either!

There were two sofas in her office, and she and I would sit facing each other while I lobbed my hopes and bogeys across the carpeted gap. The sofas were covered in leather, which slightly "bothered" my vegetarian sensibilities, although I never told her so. Perhaps my safely riding on them, steered through the perilous seas of despair, had justified whatever animals had died to cover them. Beth would have thought so. I wonder if a similar dilemma ever bothered the recipient of a medieval Bible that took the skins of two to three hundred dead sheep to make its parchment pages? After all, the Bible existed to save human souls.

People have always longed to take their dogs with them to Heaven. Victorian children had to be taught to think of Heaven as a friendly place, where, sadly, so many of their little brothers and sisters resided. Poems and stories on the subject were popular. But could the pets come too? A typical eye-dabber poem by Robert Buchanan, a nineteenth-century Scottish poet, is "The Schoolmaster's Story." A dog, Donald, always accompanies little Willie to school until Willie is caught in a snowstorm and, in spite of Donald's heroic rescue attempts, is on his deathbed:

"Do doggies gang to heaven?" Willie asked.
And ah! What Solomon of modern days
Can answer that?

In other cultures dogs themselves have sometimes been gods. Anubis was an Egyptian dog-jackal deity, with pointed ears and a long, sharp muzzle. He had the important work of calibrating whether the human heart (containing a lifetime of deeds) weighed enough to merit eternal life. The Zoroastrian Parsis considered dogs to be gods in disguise, and crimes against them were severely punished. The sacred book of the Parsis, *Zend Avesta,* devoted one volume to dogs, comparing them to priests, warriors, husbandmen, courtesans, children, and other humans. In Buddhism dogs might be reincarnations of souls that could inhabit any living creatures, not just humans.

Sothis, the Dog Star, appeared regularly at the time the Nile was to flood, leaving rich silt behind it for the new year's crops. This was in mid-July, when the land was parched. The predictable and timely appearance of floodwaters seemed like (and was) a miracle to the ancient Egyptians. The Romans also watched the Dog Star, the brightest star in the heavens, calling it Sirius, from a Greek word for "scorching." They said that Sirius had once been the mighty hunter Orion's dog, and now stayed near him. The *dies caniculares* were the "dog days" of summer, when the predawn rising of Sirius coincided with hot weather, and was believed to intensify the sun's heat. It made men lethargic and caused rabies in dogs. We still use the expression "dog days" to describe the sweltering days of summer that sap us of energy and resolve.

ROBIN DIED IN JULY. After his death, I didn't go to Quaker Meeting anymore. On Sunday mornings I usually took the dog for a walk through the woods and fields. We had Meeting by ourselves.

Care and Feeding

FOR QUITE A long time after Robin died I could barely eat, and I cooked family meals mechanically. Some things I could no longer make, like apple pie. It had been Robin's favorite. When he was in college and would telephone that he was coming home, I would start to slice apples. It was a long time before I could handle an apple. Even when avoiding the foods he had liked, every mealtime we had a vacant place at the table. My garden was a place where the memory of Robin's bright hair popped out between rows of vegetables any time I attempted to work there. I didn't cultivate the vegetables he hadn't liked, or the vegetables he had liked, for opposite and equally compelling reasons, so the depleted garden was scant comfort.

As I gradually began to take a slow interest in life, I started to garden again, to grow vegetables, to cook more creatively. Then one day, in spite of the fear that she would reject my offering, I brought Beth some vegetables from my garden.

"I don't suppose you want any of these," I muttered nonchalantly, shoving them at her. But she accepted them with enthusiasm.

Many psychologists won't accept gifts from their clients, because of that line between friendship and professionalism. Beth was firm. I couldn't be her friend. If I became her friend she wouldn't be able to help me. Why not? Friends can't be counselors. Her job, she told me, was to help *me*. Friends take turns helping each other. Ours had to be a one-sided relationship.

"Your counselor can be your friend," she said, "Your friend can't be your counselor."

Gradually, however, I became bolder, including her in my regained ability to feed my family. I made some of my vegetables into soup, and offered her that, again nervous that she would consider I had overstepped the boundaries. Again, she seemed delighted, saying she rarely cooked, her schedule being too busy, and she loved homemade soup. I started bringing her a basket at every visit, filled with flowers, soup, and anything else I thought she might enjoy. I grew bolder still, and tried to think of little gifts she might enjoy.

"Why do you want to give this to me?" she asked, when I first presented her with something better than the soup. I had a feeling this was a standard question, learned in her training.

"Well, to start with, you saved my reason, perhaps my life."

"That may not be true, anyway, it's my privilege."

Privilege. That was another word that I suspected came from a textbook. I grew impatient.

"You'd think you'd lent me your comb. Isn't my happiness worth anything?" That did it. I could give her presents. It was the best therapy of all, choosing something I thought she might enjoy. I told her, truthfully, that I needed to give her presents, because I could no longer give them to my sister. Still, I avoided going to her local church sale for fear I would find the things I had given her, and that she had accepted, for sale with the rest of the jumble.

I always felt a bit scruffy when I visited Beth, with my gardener's hands, and dog hairs on my clothes. She was personally very elegant, with lovely outfits and beautifully manicured hands. But, though elegant, she was plump, and I soon discovered that she worried about her weight.

I, who had watched my lovely plump sister shrivel and die, urged my counselor to stay the way she was.

"You're beautiful the way you are. Don't diet."

"Thanks. That's just the kind of help I don't need." I was instructed to bring "healthy" food, broccoli or vegetable soup, and no starch, in her next basket. She accepted it graciously (though Richard teasingly said she probably gave it to the dog). Luggs certainly would have eaten it, broccoli and all. He ate anything. Beth's "diets" never seemed to last very long, and I never noticed much change in her shape. This pleased me—I didn't want any more changes in my life.

Luggs was definitely overweight and had special diet food that cost (as I discovered when he was visiting and ran out of food) about the same as good-quality hamburger. It might have done him more good if he had stuck to the diet food, rather than eating the diet food in addition to anything else he could get. One time I went upstairs, and in the space of five minutes he had taken a large, warm loaf of bread off the counter and completely devoured it. It was a bit late to scold him when we missed the loaf at suppertime. Dogs, unlike people, can't feel guilty for past sins, and have to be caught *in flagrante delicto* for a reprimand to make any connection.

I enjoyed cooking, and Beth's basket began to satisfy

a nurturing instinct, which the absence of so many of my family had left unfulfilled. Baudelaire wrote of "certain sexagenarian maidens, whose deserted hearts are devoted to beasts because stupid men no longer want them." I was soon to be a sexagenarian, and my husband certainly wanted me, but there was a limit to how much food he could consume. Richard would poke into the weekly basket, licking his lips, pretending to be neglected. In fact he always got some of the contents too.

Actually it worried me that I needed a counselor at all, when I had a husband whom I dearly loved. Why did I talk to her, not to him? But far from being jealous of my devotion to her and her ability to calm me, Richard seemed glad of anything or anyone who could help me. We could not help each other, as we had always done before. Struck by the same tragedy, we seemed separate even from each other, each in a cocoon of grief. Like a bitch guarding a wounded puppy, I had protected my sorrow, allowing no one to approach me. I had slowly allowed Beth in, and I began to come alive again. Seeing her comfort me perhaps helped Richard, too.

FOR MANY PEOPLE, looking after pets fills an empty hunger, and even the privileged feel a need to nurture their pets themselves. The actress Doris Day had six housekeepers to look after her dogs, and there was a special kitchen in her California home for preparing their food. Their menu included turkey loaves, mashed potatoes, brown rice, and low-fat cottage cheese. But the actress did all the shopping for them herself and felt, it seems, that it was "the least she could do" for her pets, because they gave her back so much.

Dog owners love to feel they are doing just what is right for their pet. The dog food industry is very big business. Americans spend millions of dollars on dog food, and the pet food section in supermarkets is usually as large as that for baby food. The first manufactured dog food was the brainchild of James Spratt, who went to London, so the account goes, to sell lightning conductors, and noticed homeless dogs lurking by the docks to eat the sailors' moldy biscuits, which were thrown out at the end of a voyage. In 1860 Spratt concocted his Patent Meat Fibrine Dog Cakes, which contained wheat, beetroot, and vegetables cooked with beef blood.

When I was a child, most British households still cooked their own dog food. My job was to feed the dog. We mixed either horse or whale meat (which now of course would be considered unacceptable) with chunks of bread, and any household scraps. But in America after World War II, housewives were enjoying a new emancipation from kitchen chores. Fast food came in for humans, and commercial dog food became big business. Even though much of it was grains and vegetables, it was always advertised as "meaty," and this is still a selling point. The packaging is made to appeal to humans, because, in spite of commercials, dogs can't read the labels on the cans and boxes. Dogs have evolved to eat heartily in gulps, without tasting too carefully, because their ancestors didn't eat regularly and had to eat quickly. But we find it satisfying to give our dogs tempting-looking "hamburger" patties or "bacon bits," and we are still horrified when they lick sewage off the street.

It's not certain that dogs need meat. Victorian dog specialists thought that meat made dogs more savage, and that females could be unpleasantly "inflamed" by ingesting it. Bread and milk were often fed to them instead, or pots of vegetables mixed with a very few butchers' scraps. Sometimes puppies were even given human milk. In 1786, Samuel Johnson's friend Mrs. Thrale wrote that "it is a common thing enough for ordinary men's wives to suckle the lap-dogs of ladies of quality." In other cultures puppies were sometimes suckled by women and later used as food themselves, unless the women grew too fond of them, and kept them as pets.

Dogs that were to be eaten themselves were not fed

meat. Perhaps luckily for the succulently chubby Luggs, in our culture we don't eat dogs, although we often do eat animals that might be as intelligent as dogs. For us, dogs are members of our families, and thinking of our pets as food fills us with horror. In some countries, however, dogs were fattened for food. The Japanese Shinto religion forbade eating any land mammals, including dogs, but the Chinese bred and fattened chows for food.

In poor countries dogs still have to fend for themselves, but in rich societies pampering dogs is nothing new. In 1606 a courtier at the French court told the dauphin that he should be giving bread to the poor, not to his dog. The dauphin is said to have replied, "Are dogs rich?"

Politicians will use whatever they can, including dogs, to lend credence to their plans. In 1791, a Mr. G. Clark addressed the British parliament about levying a dog tax. Dogs, he pointed out, were unnecessary. In addition, he added sanctimoniously, they "consume provisions that children would be glad of." Dog taxes were successfully levied after the nineteenth century, but plenty of children still remained hungry.

A socially conscious friend of mine worried about the hungry people that the cost of one week's dog food in the city of New York could feed. Yet when I examined my own conscience, and tried to visualize a (no longer) hungry person sitting on my own dog's rug, I came out with a low grade. I shamefully had to admit that I didn't want anybody, however worthy, in his stead. Guiltily, I wanted my dog. Just as I wanted my therapist.

AS TIME WENT on Beth's baskets included applesauce and, finally, apple pie. I never told her what that meant.

I don't know exactly what happened that made it possible for me to make apple pie again, to see, eventually, bright blossoms, or a child in a red coat, to glimpse once more a brilliant bird, flitting through green foliage. The change came about gradually, and there was no doubt that Luggs was a part of the process. He was not a dog I would necessarily have chosen to connect with, for I had always favored quiet dogs rather than effusive ones. But Luggs, with his wonderful appetite for living, broke down my preconceptions, even about Beth.

In my former life, Beth's office, a stark new building in an empty, gray parking lot, would have depressed and discouraged me. Now it was like a fertile island in a barren sea. Her tinkling, recirculating fountain, pictures of gilded angels, books on every possible form of abuse (some of which I had never even heard of), stacks of children's games, and fluffy stuffed animals in various pastel colors would probably have induced my sarcastic scorn. Instead they became symbols of comfort. And her solid form bending over the basket, eagerly poking through it to see what treats I had brought her, made me feel something that approached pleasure.

Working Like a Dog

DOGS WILL CONTENTEDLY lie next to us for hours, snoozing or gazing into space. They are programmed to fall into a blissful stupor when nothing else is going on, although they do dream as well. In between idle hours, they give their whole attention to what they are doing. "Letting a sleeping dog lie" is no problem as far as most dogs are concerned, because they are asleep much of the time.

I used to ask Beth sometimes why "just talking" to her helped me. She just sat there, after all, and listened. Even when she gave me advice, most of it was nothing out of the ordinary, nothing that I couldn't eventually have figured out for myself. Why did I need her? When I pressed her, she said it was because she *did* listen to me. "Most of the time we don't really listen," she said. "We just wait to reply."

Listening didn't seem like work to me. But then neither did "therapy," although I knew it was commonly perceived as such. Were we both "working through" my problems? Beth, with gentleness and humor, occasionally remarked that I was "stubborn," or "always wanted to do things *my* way." (My mother would have agreed with her!) But she seemed relaxed and amused when we chatted, and I never really considered that her relaxed humor might have been a kind of work. When she went away she often said afterward that she had enjoyed her "rest."

I still didn't get it. I was talking, and she was listening. After all, Luggs listened to me too. On the other hand, Luggs felt free to doze off if I made him listen too long. Beth (as far as I observed) did not. Luggs didn't reply either, of course. If he had, I presume his advice would have been basically that of everybody else: "You can't do anything about what has happened, so you must accept it. In your place I would distract myself with a treat here and there." Good psychology? Nice dog, anyway.

Beth seemed to have endless patience to listen to my desolate whining, but, from my point of view, she would leave undone the oddest things. Outside her office door was a sadly neglected potted palm. It had completely dried out, so I used to water it on every visit, until one day, hardly thinking, I scooped it up and staggered out to the car with it. Next session I said to her, "It was me who stole your tree."

"What tree?"

I explained. She shook with laughter. I was welcome to it. I offered to bring it back after it had recovered and rested, but she urged me to keep it. I didn't really have the space for it, but I kept it anyway.

I, who so often despaired at life itself, could never have kept a vase of dead flowers in my room. But I would leave a vase of fresh flowers on Beth's table, and next week there they would be, brown and slimy in the same vase, waiting to be replaced by the new ones I brought. In vain I pleaded with her: "You can't have dead flowers in your office. You must throw them away. Suppose someone comes in to be cheered up and sees them. What will they think?"

She would smilingly protest that she had been "busy." She was at the height of her profession then, rarely having an opening for a new appointment, working for the county court as well as for individuals like myself. I knew how much time she spent at her job.

What is "work?" Once when my eldest son, Adrian, was very small, he was playing with a friend so quietly all morning that I went out to see what they were doing.

Adrian proudly showed me two piles of sand at either end of the yard, one larger than the other. He explained that they were moving the sand, and the pile they had moved was larger than the pile that was left. I, of course, congratulated them, tenderly thinking of the simplicity of children, how they had "worked" all morning on what to an adult would be an utterly pointless project. But when I told Richard, he pointed out that he had spent the morning removing chips from a block of marble, and I had probably spent some of the morning cleaning, moving "dirt" from one place to another.

Robin would never do anything he did not think worthwhile, whatever the consequences, and intentionally had himself expelled from school because he decided not to write a compulsory paper. When he did think something worthwhile, nothing could stop him. Although he had left school at sixteen, he ended up in one of the top biology labs in the country. A life of great promise was cut short. Had he decided it was not worthwhile? He was ill, Beth told me, and could not help himself. But, whatever she said, I could not be reconciled to his untimely death.

Those who do not weigh the value of everything have easier lives. When I complained about the dead flowers to Beth, I was practically accusing her of abusing the universe itself. She suffered no worries about that. She would cheerfully agree that I was quite right, and that she should have removed the dead flowers. The next week another shriveled bouquet would be there, just as before. The first thing I always did was to clear them up before we talked. I wondered whether the other clients noticed such sad flowers, or minded, if they did notice.

IF HUMANS AGONIZE over the "purpose" of life, dogs are a cheery antidote. They simply get on with the job, and if there is no apparent job for them, they go to sleep.

Although the majority of dogs are now kept as pets, in the past only the privileged kept pets, and most dogs had to help their owners, which they did willingly. This working relationship between dogs and humans seems to have developed early. Noah took two of many animals, including two dogs (breed not specified), into the ark with him. In an early demonstration of the dog's service to man, it was said that these two dogs were asked, or volunteered, to stop a sudden leak in the ark with their noses, which remained wet and cold ever after.

From earliest times dogs were kept to assist hunters. Judaism discouraged hunting, so the Hebrew people did not keep fine hunting hounds, as did early Egyptians and Arabs. Arabian hounds, similar to our greyhounds, were called salukis. Salukis were allowed into the sheik's tent, as opposed to the despised pariah dogs of Islam, called *kelb.* Salukis, named after Saluk, a town in southern Arabia that has now vanished, were never to be sold, and could only be given away as gifts.

Early hunting with these hounds was by sight. The greyhound, or *gazehound,* sees its prey, and can run incredibly fast after it. Arab hunters let "seeing hounds" loose after gazelles or hares, which were visible for miles in the open desert.

Some dogs follow their prey by scent, and were used by huntsmen to follow foxes through brush, a chase that Oscar Wilde described as "the unspeakable in full pursuit of the inedible." If the hunted animal took refuge in a burrow underground, a "terrier" (from the Latin *terra,* "earth") could dig it out.

A scent hound has about 220 million scent receptors in its nose, a human has about 5 million! A hound can detect the presence of one drop of blood in five liters of water, and can follow the trails of individuals, including identical twins. If a scent hound tracks a man who takes to a bicycle, the scent isn't lost (although taking to water or being lifted into the air will break it).

In medieval Europe, hunting was a sport for nobility, and real hunting hounds were a status symbol, jealously reserved for the elite. In 1016, the Council of Canute the Dane at Winchester decreed that "No mean person may keepe any greyhound." If a commoner kept any kind of hound or mastiff, it had to be mutilated so it could be recognizable if used to poach the king's game. Commoners' dogs were cruelly hamstrung, or the middle toes of the forefeet were lopped off, using an eight-inch-thick board for the purpose. The dog's foot was held on it, and a chisel was placed on the three middle claws to "smite them cleane off." Hounds that resembled legal hunting hounds were sometimes "curtailed" or deprived of their tails, thenceforth being known as "curs," or common, undistinguished dogs.

Dogs were sometimes bred specifically to assist in hunting birds. A "setter" would set, or crouch, waiting by the game it had rounded up, until a net could be thrown over both it and the birds. A "cocker" spaniel was used specifically to stalk woodcocks. A "springer" sprang forward. "Spaniels," or "Hispanioles," were hunting dogs introduced from Spain, or Hispania. Poodles, or "puddle" dogs, were water dogs used for duck hunting. The German dachshund was bred to hunt one particular animal, *Dachs* being a badger.

Dogs seem to enjoy being trained, even though some dogs lovers claim that learning undoggy disciplines, such as ignoring fragrant lampposts on sidewalks (as guide dogs must), is hard on them. Most hunting dogs had to be trained against their instincts. If the prey was already dead, they had to retrieve it without damage. Or they might be trained to chase and keep the prey at bay, again not killing it, until human hunters arrived to finish it off.

Labrador retrievers like Luggs were introduced to Britain in the nineteenth century. By this time guns had been developed to shoot further, so a dog was useful for finding and retrieving game, mostly ducks, that had fallen quite far away, sometimes into water. Fishermen had trained Labradors to retrieve fishing nets and ropes, and when they were first brought to Britain on cod-fishing boats, they were called Newfoundlanders, like the other large water dogs from Newfoundland. In 1885 the new British Quarantine Act forbade importing animals from abroad and at about the same time, breeding Labradors in Newfoundland was restricted because these dogs were believed to prey on sheep. The earl of Malmesbury had an estate called Heron Court near Poole Harbor, where cod boats docked. From about 1878, Lord Malmesbury had imported and bred these retrievers, later changing their name to Labrador (many fishing boats came from there to Britain). All Labradors are believed to have descended from Lord Malmesbury's and his neighbor's, the duke of

Buccleuch's, nineteenth-century dogs. "The real breed," wrote Malmesbury, "may be known by their having a close coat which turns the water off like oil, [and] above all, a tail like an otter."

Luggs, a purebred English Labrador, did indeed have a glistening oily coat and a very thick tail (which he constantly wagged). Whether he could have been trained to retrieve ducks, I do not know. You couldn't make him do much he didn't want to, although he was always charming as he ignored commands.

WE HUMANS HAVE used dogs to help us in so many ways. Dogs excel at making bonds between people and are considered good therapy for just about anybody, but particularly the old or lonely, because people tend to speak to strangers with dogs more often than they speak to strangers without dogs. Dogs are used to visit and cheer the terminally ill, as well as the severely depressed. It isn't what they do, but more probably what they don't do that helps. Emily Dickinson wrote, in 1862, that dogs are "better than human beings because they know, but do not tell." Psychologists also try to know and not tell. For some people dogs can do better.

From the time of the blind Christian St. Hervaeus, who

was led by a "seeing-eye" wolf, dogs have been trained to guide the nonsighted. Seeing Eye dogs probably use their sense of hearing and smell to guide them as much as their eyes. Now dogs are also trained to help the deaf and humans with other physical disabilities.

The original bulldog was bred to worry a bull to death. Bull baiting was considered a gastronomic necessity before it became a sport, because it was believed that the meat from a frightened animal would be more tender and nutritious. Lacking dogs, sometimes a meat animal was beaten to death. Even with this rationale, there was a Scottish tradition that butchers be precluded from jury duty, because they might be too hardhearted. The noses of bulldogs (*bouledogs* in France) were gradually bred flatter and their jaws underslung, so they could hang on to the bull's muzzle, never letting go, until, exhausted, the bull died. Today we use meat tenderizer—and keep bulldogs as pets.

Whether it's baiting bulls, hunting, or herding sheep, dogs will do it for us, and they don't question the value of what they do. Some dogs have worked for humans so far back that their skills are partly instinctive. Sheepdogs, for instance, will herd anything they can, from cars to people, if no sheep are handy.

When I was little, we had a sheepdog that herded *us* like sheep. Our Shetland sheepdog, Larry, was for me a symbol of being a family once more. When my parents finally did recover from tuberculosis enough for me to leave my grandmother in Scotland, we were reunited in England. My father could no longer work abroad in the Colonial Service, but he had a job in London. I smothered Larry with a nine-year-old's matronly affection. I not only talked to him, I dressed him in dolls' clothes and pushed him around in a perambulator. I babied him adoringly, loving him more than my own baby brother, of whom I was jealous. After my two years in Scotland, my family seemed like strangers, and, lonely as I had been, I felt displaced when I rejoined them. I quarreled energetically with my older brother. Technically Larry was his dog, given to him after a trip to the Shetland Islands, and it didn't help that I had not been included in that holiday but left behind with Granny's cook.

I never quarreled with Anna. We shared a room, and I loved having an elder sister again. Anna was strong and fun, and called me her "funny little sister." Our mother was supposedly better but still spent most of her time in bed, and we were instructed not to upset or tire her, lest she become ill again. We weren't supposed to hug or kiss either of our parents in case lingering tuberculosis might infect us.

Like all sheepdogs, Larry was extremely intelligent, and also devoted to his "flock" (ourselves). He allowed me to dress him in pink bonnets with unfailing patience, but at heart he was a herder. We lived at that time outside London, in Kent, a county famous for its apple orchards. Especially at blossom time we would walk through the extensive orchards surrounding us. The trees, planted in symmetrical alleys, met above our heads, like shell pink cathedral cloisters thick with translucent blossoms. When the petals began to fall they covered the ground thickly, and my siblings and I would pelt each other with flickering pink until they dissolved into mush. On these walks we never could resist teasing Larry by walking in a group, and then deliberately separating. He would be frantic, running around and around us, trying to herd us together, even nipping behind our heels. He had never lived with sheep, but his instincts had not been eliminated by pethood, or by pink bonnets either.

Dogs seem to love working with humans, and indeed seem worst off when they are alone and bored. A dog is as happy to chase and retrieve a thrown ball as it is to retrieve a dead duck, as happy to follow the scent of a murderer as to fruitlessly chase rabbits on a walk. In universal terms, perhaps their values are as sound as ours, after all. For who is to judge the value of a dead partridge laid at a hunter's feet against a ball returned to a child on the beach?

Where No Dog Has Gone Before

DOGS WILL FOLLOW unflaggingly wherever we take them. If we don't take them anywhere, they will wait forever. They aren't necessarily lazy. They are just waiting for whatever life will bring.

Once I romantically told Richard that I would follow him "to the ends of the earth."

"I know you would," said he, "but you'd give me a lot of aggravation about asking directions for the right way to go."

Women frequently complain that their husbands won't stop to ask directions, preferring to be lost for hours. Maybe that's why men have often taken their dogs, rather than their wives, on their journeys. A dog's home is that of his master, and dogs stick to their human companions however long the trail. Cats, even affectionate ones, don't follow people, but stay home.

In the past, when exploration was often on foot, trudging to unknown ends of the earth, dogs often kept explorers company, following them and suffering with them. In his *Travels,* Peter Kalm, who explored North America in the eighteenth century, tells of an Indian legend about the creation of the dog. God, the story went, took a stick and said to the people, "Here thou shalt have an animal which will be of great service to thee, and which will follow thee wherever thou goest." The stick then turned into a dog.

"Walkies" was a treat to Nemo and Luggs, and we always came home at the end of it, but I believed they would unconditionally have followed *me* to the ends of the earth had I demanded it of them. Even Luggs, who was fat and tired easily, would trudge after me through terrain that I knew was quite an adventure for him. He was used to sedate walks in the park, but I tugged him through brush, over logs, and across slushy fields. At first he was utterly bewildered, and he would try to get under the logs, or around streams, to avoid the exertion of jumping. But in the end he learned to jump quite well. He even stopped sitting down in passive disobedience when the going got hard. Beth said he usually slept for a couple of days when he got home. When he arrived at our house he always whined and barked until we went out into the fields and woods, which he eagerly reexamined. He was like a city child coming back to summer camp. He even had his green canvas "camp collar," which we put on as soon as he arrived, because at home he either wore no collar or a choke collar for walks. He had his own bed at our house too, and since he never remembered to bring a toilet kit, I bought him a brush.

Luggs, like myself in this new world of therapy, was exploring new territory, although mine was of the heart and mind rather than of muddy fields and woods. Hard as he found the going, I think Luggs adapted more readily than I.

But a dog is good to take along when exploring any new places, whether emotional or geographical, and many dogs have gone exploring with their masters. At the beginning of his famous journey west, Meriwether Lewis bought himself a black Newfoundland puppy. He paid twenty dollars for the dog, a large sum at the time, and refers to it quite often in his journals. The dog, Seaman, once saved Lewis's life by diverting a large buffalo that almost charged into his tent. Seaman assisted the explorers numerous times when negotiating with the American Indians they met. A dog so large and furry was quite unknown to the people of western America, and several times Lewis was asked if he would trade him. Lewis refused, because "I prised [him] much for his docility and qualifications generally for my journey." The qualifications included catching squirrels for the table. When Seaman was stolen, Lewis immediately sent a posse of three men after the thieves, ordering that if they encountered "the least resistance or difficulty in surrendering the dog to fire on them." The thieves, who knew they could be shot dead for stealing even an ax, relinquished Seaman. We don't know what happened to Seaman. Lewis made one last, rather strange, entry about him in his journal, on July 7, 1806: "My dog much worried." Then Seaman is never mentioned again.

Some explorers went quite alone except for a dog. A nineteenth-century German botanist, Eduard Poeppig, searched for orchids and other rare plants in Cuba. The *Botanical Magazine* of 1835 described Poeppig finding a particularly beautiful plant and being "compelled to relieve his full heart by uttering loud shouts of joy, to which his faithful dog, the sole companion and witness of his delight, responds by many a yelp of exultation."

Not all the dogs that went willingly on exploration trips survived. Kitchin, the dog of Joseph Hooker, the famous nineteenth-century explorer from Kew, died on a plant-exploring trip in the Himalayas, slipping off a bamboo bridge and falling into the rapids far below. "For many days I missed him," wrote Hooker sadly, "by my side on the mountain, and by my feet in the camp."

Billy, David Douglas's dog, survived but was left alone when his master died. Douglas, namesake of the Douglas fir, was a lonely Scottish explorer who had not much use for people. He even resigned from the prestigious Royal Botanical Society, calling it a "beastly club." But on his trips Douglas was always accompanied by Billy, his little terrier. Although he carried all his luggage on his back, this explorer patriotically included a suit of tartan clothes to wear whenever he reached civilization. Billy, of course, was a *Scottish* terrier. In July 1834, Douglas fell into a bull trap in Hawaii (no one knows how), and Billy was found howling at the edge of the pit in which were the explorer's gored body and the enraged bull. Douglas's death was a bit of a mystery—some say he was murdered—but the only witness, Billy, could not say what had happened. Billy had to be persuaded to leave the bull pit. He was adopted by a clerk from the British foreign office, and lived out the rest of his life in England. One imagines that Douglas would have preferred him to have lived in Scotland.

• • •

Dogs will follow us wherever we go. Even if they are exposed to danger, and even if they can't understand why we are going where we go, they don't like being left behind. In our family we mostly had to leave our dogs when we went on trips. One time, though, we did take our dog along, with nearly disastrous consequences.

When our boys were small we had a beloved and ornery dog called Rabbit. Someone had named her, before we got her, for her very large ears. She looked like a cross between a favorite toy and a jackal and, of all the dogs we had, she was the one who most loved to roll in foul-smelling carcasses. If there was one anywhere within miles she would find it, roll in it, and come home with that slightly ashamed, slightly triumphant look of a woman returning from the beauty parlor with a new hairstyle. She would then be bathed or banished, according to the weather. If we called her to be bathed, she would lie down and slither on her stomach as if her legs were paralyzed. When released, clean and fluffy as a Christmas toy, she would immediately head for the smell again. Usually we gave up and let her stay outside for a few days until it wore away. She really preferred being outside, and sometimes messed if we kept her in when her barking drove us crazy. We suspected she did it on purpose, because she certainly didn't lack intelligence. I knew why she had been taken to the dog pound, and *she* knew I would never take her back there.

As well as rolling in all things foul, Rabbit also stole our hens' eggs. It took us a long time to understand why the hens had "stopped laying," while she grew daily fatter and glossier. By the time we caught her, red-pawed, she had learned to balance an egg, bite its top neatly off, and lick out the inside without spilling. That finally explained the puzzling, almost intact eggshells we had found under a tree.

I don't think he was really serious, but Richard threatened to leave Rabbit, who came with us on a trip out west, in the desert. We were to spend the summer in New Mexico, where Richard had a sculpture commission. We traveled out there in an ancient station wagon loaded to the breaking point with three children and all our gear for several months. It took about ten days to get there, as we had to stop often with the children, the youngest, Peter, being less than a year old. The car was creaky and rusty, and I later boasted that I was the only woman who had crossed America on a pizza tray (which was covering a hole in the floor in front of my seat). But we had only one serious breakdown, in Little Rock, Arkansas, where we spent a week in a tent in the rain, waiting for a new part.

I was used to diverse emergencies, which included a ride in a police van (when the car gave out on the highway), clutching dog food and diapers. I had learned not to panic at small surprises, like observing our seven-year-old son using a different-colored toothbrush. When questioned, Chuck said he had found it in a sink in the men's room and had "traded," because he preferred that color!

Rabbit, though, tested us sorely. We had stopped in the desert for a picnic, and it was incredibly hot. We felt sorry for her because she had been in the car all morning, and we let her loose for a run. She was gone a rather long time and we had (luckily) finished our lunch before she reappeared. To say she smelled would be inadequate. No words could describe her odor. Apparently she had found some dead reptile and rolled in it. We recoiled. Richard, in exasperation, said he could not drive a car containing that smell. He threatened to leave her in the desert. We sat, holding our noses and coughing. It was burning hot, and we glared at each other and at Rabbit, who knew she had erred badly, shivering in the sand. The children howled. I threatened to divorce Richard.

We had a few bottles of water in the car, but nothing that could meet an olfactory challenge of this kind. Finally I remembered the large black garbage bags for dirty diapers. We put the dog, whole, inside one, leaving only her head out, and tied it tightly around her neck. I think she knew what was at stake because she sat quietly without struggling, her face, surrounded by its black plastic ruff, looking distinctly ashamed. It must have been terribly hot inside that plastic casing. We drove fast and silently across the desert to the nearest town, where we found a tap and bought an enormous bottle of shampoo. There was no divorce.

I HAD FOLLOWED Richard to live with him in America because I loved him. Not that this was doglike, because we had made the decision together. Even so, I still missed my family, and although my home was now in America, I still went back to England as often as I could. Anna, my mother, and I spent long days together, "catching up" on our lives, taking up where we had left off the last time. When first Anna and then, not long afterward, my mother died, I had lost more than two people. England no longer seemed to be home. Without Anna to welcome me, there seemed little point in going back for visits. I felt, as I had never felt before, that I was in a foreign country, not only the foreign country of my grief but an actual new land that would have to be my *only* home now. I had lost my roots.

If only I could have forgotten what I had lost. If only I

could have curled up where I did have a home and food, and people who loved me still. If only I could truly have found a new sister in Beth. It was hard not to feel wistful when she came back from a vacation with her sisters.

Do dogs live in the present, unconcerned about their past, eagerly following? And if so, and we could be more like dogs, would therapists find themselves out of business? Or would some of us still be wandering, lost in life, still needing to ask directions to the ends of the earth?

Being Heard

LIKE MOST DOG lovers, I consistently tried to bridge the species gap between me and my dogs, talking to them as if they could understand me, and partly believing that they did. As for Luggs, when I chatted to him, was I really talking to a dog, or to his connection with Beth?

I did find my therapist's dog more rewarding than her answering machine. Her recording could be reached day and night, and many a wakeful night, when I was chased by dark memories, I would listen to it. First she would cheerily announce, "Hello. This is Dr. Beth Johnson." Well, it wasn't. It was a recording of a voice, which is not at all the same as being a person, and really not even as good as a warm dog on the bed.

I would listen to Beth's voice, asking me to "leave a

message, taking as long as you like." At first I merely listened silently, and it did help to anchor me into sanity again. But when I told her this, she said she wanted to know who was calling in at 3 A.M. So I would identify myself, adding always, "You don't have to reply." Typically, I was disappointed that she took me at my word.

"You called me several times in the night last week. You must have been awake a lot," she would say.

"You didn't call back," I would complain.

"You told me not to. I can't read your mind, you know."

Nowadays people have to leave their dogs for extended periods while they go to work. Dogs are social animals and prefer to be with somebody all the time. Dog owners can purchase a machine that records their own voice and is reactivated every time the lonely dog comes near it. Apparently this soothes dogs, but are they fooled?

Beth's voice somewhat soothed me in the empty night. But it was only a machine, and machines can't answer our needs, however well they imitate us. Dogs can't "answer" us either, although they can, and do, give us mute comfort. While it is true that humans can't read each other's minds—and perhaps it's just as well—I suspected that Luggs, if he had been able to, would have called me back, whether I had actually asked him to or not.

And how important is the reply? Mothers chatter to their babies, and modern science says that, reply or not, it's an essential part of their relationship. Conversing without expecting a reply was not new to me. I had talked to my unconscious, dying mother for weeks, hoping she heard me, but she did not respond. Then, just before she died, I reminded her of a magical walk that she, Anna, and I had been on together. English bluebells filled the woods, knee high in sheets of quivering sapphire flowers on either side of a narrow path. Anna went first, then Mum, and then me, following their silent backs and bowed heads. For once we were not laughing and gossiping, as if we instinctively knew that this was an eternal moment.

"Remember the bluebell walk with Anna?" I asked my mother's inert body. "Remember?" Then, at last, just once, she squeezed my hand before she, next in line, passed on.

WE LONG TO know we've been heard. Manifesting this need, ancient legends have humans talking to animals and everyone understanding exactly what was going on. Christian saints were said to have talked to other creatures and been understood. But they were almost always giving orders to protect humans or improve their own lives. St. Thelka was caged with a lion that she dissuaded from attacking her. A medieval jackdaw was excommunicated after stealing an abbot's ring, and died of "shame." The bishop of Trier banished swallows from his cathedral, because their twittering disturbed devotions and their droppings soiled church vestments. It was said that thereafter any swallow entering the cathedral would die, and apparently none dared. In these stories the creatures not only understood commands but also the purpose of the commands, and seemed to think in *human* ways, or in ways humans wished them to think.

The most famous saint who talked to animals was St. Francis, who called all creatures Brother or Sister, and verbally persuaded a wolf not to eat the inhabitants of a village (after he had removed a thorn from its paw). The wolf sealed the contract in front of all the villagers by shaking a paw with the saint, much as a pet dog does nowadays! St. Jerome took a thorn out of the paw of a lion who afterward became his tame companion. These stories somewhat reflect our perceived relationship with dogs: We help them in ways they cannot help themselves, and in return they refrain from hurting us, and oblige us with their doggy services. But if this is an honest pact, might not the dogs' terms be different, and include more options in choosing the course of their lives with us?

At least to a certain extent, we *can* change the course of a dog's life, or indeed our own, but no one, as I was forced to learn once again, can deflect misfortune.

One day I arrived cheerily at Beth's office with flowers and soup and candy (it was just before Easter), and I knew at once that something was wrong.

"Sit down, I have something to tell you."

In my first babyish panic I thought she was going to tell me that she was moving, giving up her practice, no longer could, or would, see me. No, it was not that.

She had breast cancer.

"Lots of people have cancer, and get well. They do. Look at me," I said. As Beth knew, I had had breast cancer myself, but so shortly before Robin had begun to show signs of depression and Anna had become desperately ill, it had been pushed to one side. And I had recovered.

I told Beth about all the women I knew who were leading full lives, years after treatment. I was almost impatient when she shook her head doubtfully. This was inflammatory cancer, she said. It was different, and the prognosis was not as good.

"But I'm not giving up," she added. She outlined the plans for treatment. She would be, she said, "in the office" as much as possible. I still could call her. I still could leave a message on her machine. She hoped I would take care of Luggs when she and Paul were "occupied" with her illness.

Not giving up? Me neither, I told her. Then I remembered Anna, and her long struggle with cancer. My courage failed, and, like a little dog, I tried to shelter behind the strength I had known. Mary Queen of Scots had a little white Maltese terrier that stayed with her in prison, and was with her when she was executed on February 8, 1587. After Mary was beheaded, the dog was discovered by the executioners, hiding under her skirt. It would not budge even when dragged out, but cowered between her shoulders, soon becoming spattered with her blood. Although the executioners had orders to destroy all things splashed with Mary's blood (in case they should become relics for her supporters), they did spare the dog, who was washed and eventually sent to France.

In our relationship Beth had accepted responsibility for helping me, and even though this time *she* was the one in bad trouble, I sat on her sofa, cowered and wept, and, as usual, she comforted me. I was still depending on Beth to tame my grief, which had always, until now, seemed to be her concern. The art of taming, however, forms a bond between tamer and tamed, a bond like that between dog and human, or as in Antoine de Saint Exupéry's *The Little Prince,* between a wild fox and a child.

In the book the wild fox tells the child, "If you tame me, then we shall need each other. . . . If you want a friend, tame me." A gap between a fox and a human prince is crossed, and they become friends. When the little prince has to go away, the fox weeps. The little prince says it is the fox's own fault: "I never wished you any sort of harm; but you wanted me to tame you."

When they part, the fox tells the little prince, "You become responsible, forever, for what you have tamed," and the little prince promises he will remember, but they must still part:

"But now you are going to cry!" said the little prince.

"Yes, that is so," said the fox.

"Then it has done you no good at all!"

"It has done me good," said the fox, "because of the color of the wheat fields."

Because of Beth, I too could now see color in the wheat fields. I had become inextricably linked to her, and indeed she to me. But now I feared she might leave me. And how I cried!

Still I tried to believe with a blind—what is called dogged—faith that she would be cured. She, too, intended to be cured. So, for the purposes of our relationship, we tacitly agreed that she would get well, if only because *I* needed *her*. Her own reasons for not wanting to die were surely nothing to do with our professional agreement. We kept the "appointments" as much as possible, and I think it gave us both a sense of security.

Once, though, she was late, and I was upset.

"I thought something had happened to you," I whined.

It turned out that she had been taking a nap, and it was the only time I can remember her being angry with me.

"You are *making* something happen to me in your mind," she snapped. Who could blame her? She had made the effort to drive to her office especially to see me, and I acted like a spoiled puppy.

She, in turn, kept reassuring me that it was "all right" if I became "angry" with her. For being ill? Counselor and counseled, we leaned across a chasm of sadness, each trying to deal with it in the way we knew.

It wasn't that I couldn't do it. I had laughed with my sister through her cancer, I had held my dying mother's hand, I had watched my father take his last breath. I had even survived losing a child. But in our connection, *Beth* had been the strong one.

Even so, I tried to be stronger. I told her that she was not well, that she should rest. That I need not see her. She, however, would have none of it.

"*I* have to see you. I *have* to come to my office. Otherwise, I'll feel useless."

"You'd never be useless. I need you."

So we continued the appointments. Once she asked me if I was "making allowances" for her, by not telling her my worries. I said I had no worries, life was pretty good right then. How could I tell her of my worry that she might not live? I no longer left messages on her machine. How could I tell her that I ached in the night because she might die, that I wanted her comfort because I felt unable to help *her*?

Some nights, wild with sorrow, I howled at the universe, like a dog howling at the moon. John Caius, who in the sixteenth century wrote *Of British Dogs*, said another name for a dog was a "Mooner," because dogs spend the night "bawing and mawing at the moon," just as wolves, their wild relatives, howl in the moonlight.

In these nights of despair I rediscovered Richard's comfort. It was he whom I now woke and who mutely comforted me. He did not even know Beth, so my sorrow was not, as with Robin, his as well. This time I could lean on him without fear of pulling him down into his own abyss. Why did I mourn so, he asked, because she had an illness from which many recovered? I could help her best by hoping. It was my turn, he reasoned, to be there for her now. He was thinking of her as my friend, not my "therapist," and naturally I would best help my friend by being cheery and strong and not dwelling on my own fears.

Could the dependent client hope to help the supportive counselor? She had redirected my life. We were used to that relationship, just as a dog is the one who is fed and looked after by its human owner. If we changed, what would happen to the connections we had worked out between us? She still wanted to be my therapist; I still wanted to be her client. Yes, even her "client," by then. I wanted her under any name! In the night, longing to call her, I wept at my helplessness, and perhaps at hers, too.

Denial

I REMAINED BETH'S client. I tried to remember Anna's illness, and the ways we had sought to help her: optimism, even if I wept in the night; little gifts, but nothing too permanent; warm soup, bright flowers. I still told Beth my "problems," but I tried to keep them whimsical like my offerings, steering always well clear of thunderous eternity. Now we had a new difference between us, one that I had experienced before. Not patient and doctor, not dog and human, but that of the critically ill and the well. We had new boundaries of evasion.

Beth's cancer, like Anna's, had periods when it was better or worse. Sometimes she did come to the office and seemed almost her old self. Sometimes there would be a message that she wasn't well enough to keep her appointment, and I brought the soup and flowers to her house, and came inside to see her too. It was strange to see the little things I'd given her around the house. So she hadn't given them away to her church sale!

Luggs was delighted when I came to their house. "He hasn't stopped wagging his tail since you came in," said one of Beth's sisters, who had come to nurse her after a period in the hospital. For Luggs, the puzzlement of separate worlds must have been eased some. He, like me, must have found it hard to live two lives, so intimate and so divided.

Yet his own world had been overturned. These days he came to my house more than ever. He accepted his altered routines, but once, when Beth unexpectedly had to go to hospital, instead of eagerly wagging his tail when I came to collect him, he refused to get into the car. I coaxed him.

"Come on, sweetheart. We're going to go walkies. We're going to have a biscuit." No fool, he sat there until I levered him bodily into the car. He whined the whole way home, and I cried too. He was uneasy during the visit, even though he seemed to enjoy it. I took him on exactly the same walk every day. We stopped at the same trees. He drank from the stream at the same spot. I, too, found this oddly soothing.

We can't hide the truth from dogs. Dogs seem to know at once who dislikes them. They can sense a quarrel in the house, or good news. Or bad news. When Robin died, we didn't at first understand that it had affected our dog. Nemo couldn't have personally missed Robin, who was not living at home by then, but the mood of the house was on him, too, even if we didn't recognize his perceptions. We only acknowledged them when Nemo himself was almost killed.

It was one of those summer evenings that stun you with loveliness, cool and soft after a hot day. It was very shortly after our world had crashed. Richard and I were sitting on the screened porch with the dog, as we often did. Outside was the dusky lawn, where our little boys had chased fireflies, played ball, tumbled, and laughed. Robin's impish face seemed to peep behind every tree he had climbed, his shadowy form flitting through the dimming light. The beauty of the evening seemed only to jeer us with throbbing, torturous reminders.

"We have to get out," one of us said. We took to our bicycles, not really heading in any direction, and the road was very busy with homegoing commuter traffic. Suddenly we heard cars honking, brakes squealing. There, standing motionless in the middle of traffic, seeming not to know where to turn, was Nemo, Nemo the dog who never ventured into the road, who always went into his kennel when we got out the bikes. Traffic was backed up along each side of him, and he stood there motionless on the darkening road, as if lost. We turned, weaving through the lights and honking cars to get to him in time. One of us held him, and the other went to get the car.

Nemo had never followed our bikes before, and he never did again. It was hard though to see him accepting our grief as his grief, too, when we could not even explain to him what had happened. He needed to be near us most of the time, and we had to watch him mourning in his own way, with no understanding except sympathy for us.

ONE WAY OF dealing with the unacceptable is by refusing to acknowledge it. A famous dog, an Akita named Hachiko, belonged to Dr. Eisaburo Ueno, a professor at Tokyo University in the 1920s. Every evening Hachiko met her master at the subway station. One day, however, the professor was not on the train. He had died at work. But Hachiko continued to meet her master every night for ten years, until she, too, finally died in 1934, aged thirteen. She had become so famous, a memorial was built for her at the station exit.

When Robin was quite small, he waited for weeks for his father to return from a sculpture commission in Italy.

It was a long time for a child, and we all missed Richard. One morning Robin announced he was going to build a flying machine. I think he intended to go and see his father in it. He found a large, empty cardboard box that had been kept closed with two flapped lids. It took the whole morning for him to thread strings through the lids so he could flap them up and down like wings. He then announced that he was about to set off, and would we all come and watch him. He explained that he would fly across the lawn, circle a large tree, and then return. He began to flap the cardboard wings vigorously up and down.

Somehow I truly expected him to take off, and could almost see the fragile cardboard box, piloted by the bright-headed child, soaring up across the lawn and around the pine tree.

We waited. Robin flapped the cardboard wings. I began to worry he would be frustrated and upset. He slowed down, his face perplexed. He then announced that he would need to do a little more work on his project. He would tie balloons onto the corners of the box, and possibly make a propeller. He had not yet learned to write, but that night he dictated a letter to his father telling him how he had made a flying machine that didn't quite work, but would very soon be flying.

The balloons didn't work either, and neither did the

propeller, but the box remained on the lawn, never abandoned, until finally the rain turned it to a mush of cardboard with four flat red balloons lying on the grass beside it. Then Richard came home, and the children were busy with other things.

The pine tree is there still, and even now I can sometimes see that box loaded with an earnest child flapping its vestigial wings. It makes its way up and around the dark branches, a little lopsided, but aloft all the same. Then it comes back to me, as I watch and wait.

Robin always believed that he could fly above reality. Sometimes his dreams made him reach new heights, sometimes his refusal to see reality got him in trouble. When his driver's license was suspended, he drove anyway. He bought himself a motorcycle. There was nothing *we* could do about it; he was grown. When stopped by the police for speeding he was asked for his license, his insurance, and his registration. Laughing, he described to his father and brothers the policeman murmuring "negative" to every question, as he laboriously recorded it in his ticket book. Robin continued to ride the motorcycle as before. *I* was not told the story until after he had died. They were afraid his mother would be more worried than amused.

At the funeral, one of his professors, praising his brilliance, said that Robin had jumped for the stars, and had only just missed touching them. I always wanted to believe that my Robin never, even at the end, lost his belief in flight.

Therapists like Beth try to steer us between accepting reality and losing our faith in miracles. When she became ill, I had to pretend she would recover. I wonder now if she herself was torn between wanting to warn me and not destroying hope, her own or mine. Perhaps even her own profession could not solve that dilemma. So we compromised. We kept to the pattern we had known before. Later I wondered if I should have howled at *her,* rather than at the moon. Perhaps, like Luggs, I should have refused to board the vehicle of our pretense. If I had smashed the boundaries between us, would it have helped either her or me?

YOU CAN KID yourself, and others, in lots of ways. After she became ill, Beth no longer wore the perfume I had associated with her. In the early days when I first went to her, she had often made remarks such as, "I like your perfume," or "That's a pretty sweater." She was, as I realized in retrospect, encouraging me to take pleasure in my appearance, as a way of pulling me out of depression, and I suspect she would have searched for ways of complimenting me whatever I wore, or however I smelled!

She herself had worn a very individual perfume, which I had never come across before. Doglike, as soon as I smelled it, I used to feel calmer, and sometimes it would linger on my clothes after I had sat in her closed little office. It became for me an evanescent comfort. I didn't know what the perfume was, but one time, waiting in the airport duty-free shop before a trip with nothing better to do, I began testing the display perfumes. There was hers! Beth was suddenly present. I saturated my handkerchief from the testing bottle (it was expensive stuff). I had thought it would comfort me on my journey, which was to see my dying mother. A handkerchief saturated with Beth's essence would be a way of taking her along with me too, to help me.

Far from it. I had soon discovered that without its proper connection, without Beth's kind smile and her gray head nodding in sympathy, the scent was actually displeasing, emphasizing the reality that she was not really near me. Like a disappointed pup, suddenly forced to recognize that the garment smelling of its mistress isn't the same as the actual loving mistress, I saw that my handkerchief was going to give me no sustenance, and I abandoned it on the plane seat. When I arrived in London, I went alone to hold my mother's hand.

That time I had managed not to kid myself, but I certainly wasn't above kidding others. On the return trip from London, I had in my suitcase some seeds of the opium poppies my mother had always grown in her garden. Although not normally a smuggler, I was determined to take them to sow in my own garden, in remembrance of her. We used to tease her about them when anyone felt indisposed, suggesting she make tea of them. She had always pretended not to know what we were talking about, protesting they were not "real" opium poppies (despite their name, *somniferum*).

While I was retrieving my suitcase from the baggage claim, I noticed a very cute little dog sniffing amongst the luggage. I approached it, hand outstretched, cooing "Good, dog, good dog."

Its owner, however, far from being pleased that I liked his dog, glared at me, and moved away. It was then that I realized the man on the end of the leash was a customs inspector. And I remembered almost at the same time the seeds in my suitcase! The customs officer clearly didn't want sentimental dog-loving ladies interfering with his work, and pulled his dog to the other end of the baggage line. I, still smiling sweetly at him from afar, picked up my case and made a pretty swift exit.

How I regretted that I could not tell my mother the story. But maybe she, being my mother, would have been more worried at my lawlessness than amused. Beth, however, had enjoyed it. The poppies came up for several years, until they finally died out.

Self-Esteem

UNLIKE MOST OTHER women of her age that I know, Beth had thick gray hair, which she did not dye. This added to the respect I felt for her. She was only a few years older than I, but my family was slow to go gray, and I perceived her as wiser and more mature than myself. I admired the way she did not try to appear younger than she was, a manifestation of the confidence in herself that had made it natural for me (and others) to be guided by her. Of course, her beautiful gray hair, which had made me feel "mothered," fell out when she underwent chemotherapy.

I made hats for her and gave her pretty scarves. There was a particular style of hat she liked, and I made it in several colors. She wore a wig for church, and to see clients, but, like my sister Anna, she sometimes allowed me to see her as she was, with no hair.

Both Anna and Beth knew that I did not think them a jot less beautiful without their hair. Indeed, my dearest memory of Anna had been when, one wonderful day, she was well enough for us to go to the beach together. Hatless, she bobbed up and down in the waves, laughing, round-headed like a little seal, and I loved her so much that I furtively cried salt tears into the salty sea.

It's funny that hair in the right or wrong places seems to be aesthetically so important. More than that, we seem actually repulsed by hair when it isn't where it should be or when it *is* where it should be. Bearded women or bald men often feel bad about themselves. Bald women fear they might embarrass those who meet them in the street. We expect some creatures to be with hair, and some to be without, and deviations, like hairless dogs, can make us uneasy.

Hairless dogs, unaware of our preconceptions, aren't self-conscious and like to be caressed. Maybe they worry us partly because we associate their condition with mange, a dangerous canine disease. The name for the human disease of hairlessness is *alopecia,* which comes from the Greek *alopex,* or "fox," and refers to a fox with mange. In the past, mangy dogs were put into foxes' burrows to control the wild fox population by spreading mange, which is highly contagious.

Most of us prefer to think of dogs as furry, and thus cuddly. You take something soft to bed, beginning in infancy with a teddy bear. If your partner becomes bald (and is not bearded), you may end up with something less furry before you are through. Funnily enough, though, in some cultures the recommended animal to take to bed for comfort was a *hairless* dog.

Hairless dogs go back so far that historians argue over their origins. Explorers to South America found them there and brought them home. The seventeenth-century compte de Buffon, who studied the animals of the New World, comparing them (usually unfavorably) with those of the Old World, said, with confidence, that hairless dogs (which he called a "degenerate species") had developed because of the hot climate. In the Mayan and Toltec cultures, chocolate-colored Xolos (hairless dogs) were, appropriately, sacrificed to the god of chocolate. Hairless dogs are found in China, too, and their evolution seems to have little to do with climate.

Not all "hairless" dogs are hairless. Some have a tuft of hair on their heads or on the end of their tails, and some even have full coats. The gene that causes hairlessness can also cause defects, such as missing teeth. The more hairy "hairless" dogs are often bred with the completely bald ones to reduce risk of genetic defects. Hairless dogs have a high body temperature (about 104 degrees Fahrenheit), and in all countries where they are found they were used medicinally, like a hot water bottle, to soothe all ailments, even toothache. One of their names was "fever dogs." Another South American name meant "dog without vestments" *(caa-allepo),* reflecting a kind of naturalness, as if they were merely unclothed like us at bedtime.

I've never known a bald hairless dog, but those who love them think them beautiful, and say they are loyal, playful, and intelligent, just like most other dogs. And of course these dogs also return love to those who love them. Even so, a lot of people don't think of them as truly doggish.

On the whole, we have consistent ideas about what is a beautiful dog—or a beautiful person. This doesn't preclude people from considering dogs that don't conform to the usual standards as beautiful too. People sometimes choose dogs to enhance the individuality of their own looks. They might select a particularly handsome dog to compensate for their own less conventional good looks. But once we love, the object of our love is beautiful, regardless, whether it be human or dog. Indeed, being thought beautiful is the surest way of becoming beautiful. As psychologists tell us, self-esteem goes a long way in persuading the world we are good to know, and to look at, too.

Luggs was fat, which gave him a rather charming clumsiness, at least to my eyes. Others might have said he waddled. I don't know if it was actually so, or I was making a wishful link with Beth, but one time when we were out walking, I remarked to Richard that Luggs looked a lot like Beth. Richard, who did not know Beth, stopped, astonished.

"I thought you said Beth was beautiful."

Just as the desirability of plumpness varies in human cultures, very big or very small dogs have been considered more attractive by humans at various times. Dogs were sometimes fed special food in the hopes of keeping them small. The sixteenth-century naturalist Ulisse Aldrovandi wrote that puppies nursing "nearest the heart" of their mother turned out big; those furthest away remained small. John Gerard wrote in his famous *Herbal* of 1597 that daisies "given to little dogs with milke, keepeth them from growing great."

The nineteenth-century explorer Robert Fortune recorded Japanese chins (which were bred from Chinese lion dogs, imported along with Buddhism) being dwarfed "by the use of saki." He added that humans liked the drink too! Chins were bred with a "butterfly head, sacred vulture-feathered feet and chrysanthemum tails." A black spot on a white forehead was desirable and said to represent the Island of Japan surrounded by the sea.

The Chinese produced the original lion (or Pekingese) dogs, sometimes calling them "under-the-table-dogs" (tables were low), or "sleeve dogs," because they were often carried in the capacious sleeves of the silk robes worn by those at court. Stealing one of these small dogs, kept to embellish aristocratic ladies, was punishable by death.

The more these dogs resembled lions (or the contemporary Chinese idea of lions), the more they were esteemed, because the lion was associated with Gautama Buddha, symbolizing his subordination of the fiercest passions. The dogs were selected carefully for their flat faces, and their noses were massaged or even broken to make them shorter. The puppies were underfed and kept cramped in baskets—a strategy similar to binding women's feet. In the imperial court, slaves held puppies for hours, massaging their limbs to keep them short.

During the reign of the Dowager Empress Cixi (aka Tzu Hsi), the diet of her treasured Pekingese dogs included sharks' fins, curlews' livers, breast of quail, antelope milk, and tea "brewed from the spring buds" of a bush from a nearby province. Those with a white blaze on the forehead were particularly valued because Gautama Buddha himself had had a white "third eye" on his forehead. The dowager empress mistakenly took the birth of a puppy with a white spot on its forehead as an omen that the Boxer Rebellion would be successful. Before fleeing from her palace, the empress had most of her Pekingese dogs killed, rather than let them fall into the hands of the Anglo-French forces. But a few were left with the empress's old aunt (who was also forgotten and left behind), and these were taken back to Britain. One of these little dogs was presented to Queen Victoria. It was named Looty (because it was war loot), a self-congratulatory symbol of Imperial Britain's confidence.

People tend to want their animals, and their gods, to look as much like themselves as possible. Pekingese dogs are very popular, quite probably because their flat faces and wide-apart eyes give them an almost human appearance. Many children are raised with storybook animals that talk and wear clothes, just as *they* do. Cartoon characters emphasize the large eyes and flat faces we find so appealing in ourselves, and cartoon animal heroes will often have "educated" accents, while cartoon rogues have "inner city" accents.

Some people even try to make dogs look more like

humans by dressing them like children. Canine catalogs include inventories of dog accessories to fit every occasion and enhance the image of their owners. This isn't new. In nineteenth-century France, the "chien de fantaisie" was clothed and coiffed, taught to walk on two legs, and sometimes wore outfits to coordinate with that of its owner. Fashions for dogs and their mistresses included sailor suits for the beach, and even a traveling suit complete with a small pocket for the dog's train ticket.

MY FAMILY HAD always lived in the country with lots of space, and tended to have the bigger, tougher dogs that fitted our lives. I never owned a "toy" dog, but I do confess to a personal prejudice against Pekingese dogs.

The only Pekingese I ever knew belonged to the housemistress at the boarding school, where I was sent soon after coming home from Scotland. My parents had found it hard to manage the dreamy independence I had acquired in Scotland. I wanted only to play with Larry, our sheepdog, or mooch around the garden, and I was often late for school or didn't do my homework. Soon after I had supposedly resettled with my family in Kent, my parents decided I needed the discipline of one of the strictest boarding schools in the country.

In boarding school I was constantly in trouble. On the hockey field I would nervously and unsportingly duck if a ball came near me. I would forget to change into my "indoor" shoes. I was found making daisy chains when I should have been fielding cricket balls. I was untidy. I was late. Sin of sins, I was caught reading a novel (instead of the Bible) during "Prayer Hour." As everybody made it clear, I couldn't seem to do anything right. I pretended I did not care, but I longed to be good at games, admired and popular. My self-esteem was not high.

The girls were terrified of the housemistress, whom we called Mrs. T. She was a large woman with red painted nails, and she, along with a matron we called "Jack" (who had a permanent nervous twitch in her cheek), ran a tight ship. I do not know, even in retrospect, what their relationship was to each other, but both Mrs. T. and Jack doted on a Pekingese dog called Winston, after the prime minister, although by then, as Mrs. T. lamented, we had a Labor government.

I was often sent to the housemistress's room to be scolded. Mrs. T., increasingly agitated at her inability to penetrate my sullenness, would elaborate on my sins, predict a dire future for me, inform me how disappointed in me my parents were. Although I was certainly not unaffected by this belittling, I was determined not to be reduced to tears. So I would fix my attention on Mrs. T.'s heaving bosom and count the pearly buttons on the tightly closing pastel cardigans she favored. Blocking out her querulous voice, I would divide or multiply those buttons, or even mentally scale a trembling path up her curves. Meanwhile, Winston would sniff and snuffle around my ankles, damply dribbling into my socks. I have disliked Pekingese dogs ever since.

Sorting It Out

WHAT HAPPY FAMILY is complete without a dog? That's often why presidents are photographed with their dogs, showing the public they are nice regular guys, as trustworthy as neighbors. Sometimes presidents favor a certain breed, which subsequently can become popular. Or, as did President Clinton, who decided on Buddy (a Labrador retriever like Luggs), a president might choose a popular breed, a link with potential voters. Theodore Roosevelt had several dogs, amongst which was a little mongrel named Skip, who reflected his image as a man of the people. Roosevelt, a rugged, "outdoor" president, found and adopted Skip on a hunting trip. Skip, the president said, was a "little dog," meaning, he explained, "a little of this and a little of that."

The oddest-looking dog we ever adopted was Ruffy. I had not intended to get another dog when he came into our lives. It was just after Peter, our youngest child and ten years younger than Robin, was born. I had accompanied a friend to the pound to help her select a new dog. She chose an elegant long-haired retriever. While I was waiting for her to fill out the adoption papers, I wandered around the pound with Peter in my arms. In a dark corner of an obscure pen was the thinnest, scruffiest, largest dog you could imagine. I stopped. He came to the fence, looked at us, and wagged his tail. I looked at him. He wagged back.

"All right," I said, "I'll take you home." I called Richard.

"You don't need to tell me," he said when he heard my voice. "You've seen a poor old dog. And you want to bring it home. I probably can't stop you anyway. So go ahead."

"He's not old." I said. "He's sad."

"Then you really *had* better bring him home," said Richard. "What's his name?"

The telephone was greasy, and there were several animal hairs attached to it. I held it not too close to my mouth.

"Ruffian." I had seen a label on the cage.

"Ruffy? That's a nice name. Well, I'll see you and Ruffy later. Don't leave Peter behind!"

So he became Ruffy.

Ruffy's ancestry was much mixed, but clearly included German shepherd and golden retriever. He seemed to have chosen (or had thrust upon him) those characteristics of both breeds that would have caused them the least vanity. He was a muddy, darkish shepherd color, rather than the beautiful gold of retrievers. His retriever ears were floppy, and fitted strangely to his huge head with its pointed shepherd nose. He was very large, and not particularly graceful.

When I told the woman in charge at the pound that I would like to take him home, she reacted unexpectedly. That dog wasn't house-trained, she said, and besides he would probably wander. He had spent his life in a farmyard, tied up. He hadn't been a family dog. Was I sure I wanted him? Yes, I wanted him. I said I would keep him tied so he wouldn't wander, and he could sleep outside. In that case, the woman informed me, she would have to send an inspector to make sure my kennel was adequate. They would send someone the day after tomorrow. I went back to Ruffy, and told him to be patient.

Richard didn't let me down. He made a very long dog

run between two large trees. The inspector came, and I was allowed to fetch Ruffy. The woman at the pound rather ominously wished me "good luck" as I led him out. I took Ruffy straight to the vet, who was not impressed, telling me he had seldom seen as many things wrong with a single dog. Ruffy had mites in his ears, his ribs showed, he had worms, he had kennel cough. He needed to be neutered.

The vet did his best, and Ruffy came home. He used his run for about a week. He wasn't going to run away, not he! He attached himself to little Peter, who was only a few months old.

Richard's aunt, who excelled in recounting gory tragedies, warned me to keep Ruffy away from Peter. She had several stories to tell (all very grisly) about small babies and large dogs. Ruffy and I took no notice. Ruffy didn't come inside (and never felt truly comfortable indoors to the end of his life), but he would wait outside for me to park the baby buggy, with Peter sleeping in it, under a tree. He would then lie down by the buggy, practically touching its wheels, and not move until I took the baby inside again. Every fine morning, Peter and Ruffy slept outside under the trees. Later the playpen was set on the lawn, with Ruffy lying next to it. Once, when Peter had started to crawl, I watched, about to intervene, as he suddenly made his way over to the huge dog, who was gnawing a bone. Ruffy stood back and waited for the baby to examine the bone and move on, and then started gnawing it again with his huge teeth.

Sometimes I used to think of Ruffy tied up in that farmyard from which he came. It seemed he could never be grateful enough for having a family. He indefatigably retrieved balls for Robin and Chuck in warm weather, and hockey pucks all winter. Every morning he went down the lane with them to wait for the school bus. Every afternoon he was there waiting for the school bus to arrive home. His very last morning, Ruffy slowly accompanied Peter, then in high school, to the bus, returned to the back door, lay down, and died.

RUFFY, LIKE MOST of the dogs we ever had, was distinguished for his soul, not his pedigree. But even expensive pedigreed dogs can end up in the pound if they don't fit their owners' lives.

Breeds of dog, like the shape of our own bodies or the length of our skirts or our own hair, go in and out of fashion. Whether we know it or not, how we want to look, what we do, what we buy, is partly shaped by those around us. And our dogs are no exception. Hundreds of children, including my little son Peter, wanted a Dalmatian after seeing the movie featuring 101 adorable cartoon Dalmatians.

Who can resist a lovable characteristic in a favored breed, such as the floppy ears of certain breeds described so touchingly by Theseus in *A Midsummer Night's Dream*? His hounds, he said, were of a "Spartan kind," and "their heads are hung / With ears that sweep away the morning dew." Owners of spaniels and hounds know exactly what that means, when they take their dogs for an early-morning walk.

The idea of true breeds is, however, relatively new in dog history. Dogs weren't sorted into breeds, at least according to their appearance, until the nineteenth century. In the past, different dogs might be imported from abroad, and a new exotic dog would soon become popular with the rich and noble: "We Englishmen are marveilous greedy gaping gluttons after novelties and covetous cormorants of things that be seldome, rare, strange and hard to get," wrote John Caius, regarding a dog newly introduced from France. In *Of British Dogs,* Caius listed only sixteen known varieties of dog. Spaniels, pomeranians, mastiffs, and hounds are seen in paintings of this time.

Linnaeus classified dogs (as he did the rest of the natural world), and in 1776 came up with a list of the different dogs of his time. They included the domesticated dog, the wise dog, the greyhound, the mastiff, the water dog, the pet dog, the Egyptian dog, the rubbing dog, and the weasel dog. The dogs were differentiated more by their habits and uses than by their looks.

In the nineteenth century, with the beginning of dog "shows," the *appearance* of the different breeds became increasingly important. The first recorded dog show was on June 28, 1859, at Newcastle-on-Tyne. It was organized by a Mr. Shorthose and a Mr. Page, and was for sporting breeds only. The judge, an expert on sporting dogs, was known as Stonehenge. About fifty dogs were entered.

In 1863 the first large dog show was held at Chelsea, and was harshly criticized because inadequate drinking facilities had been provided for the contestants. In 1874 things were better organized, and the *Kennel Club Stud Book* was published. This named forty different breeds, and required proper registration of the competitors. By the end of the century, shows were patronized by royalty, including the elegant borzois of the Russian czar, and subsidized by the new dog biscuit manufacturers. Until his death in 1939, Charles Cruft (formerly a salesman for Spratt's "dog cakes") was the most important person behind dog shows, and by the time he died there were over nine thousand entries at the Cruft's dog show.

As dog breeding became more and more refined, only specific colors and markings were permitted in certain dog breeds. A new, exclusive breed sometimes arose from a single mutant pup. The original golden retriever is thought to have been a single gold pup born to a black mother in 1901. Lord Tweedmouth, the owner of the mother, bred and rebred the pup (named Nous), crossing it with setters and water spaniels, until he established the line.

Rules became rigid. Cocker spaniels could have a wide variety of colors and markings *but* they had to be "A.S.C.O.B." (meaning "Any Solid Color Other than Black"). English cocker spaniels, if of a solid color, could only have white on the chest! Why? For the same reason that Samoyeds could only be white or cream, Dalmatians had to be symmetrically spotted, and certain dogs had to have ears that pricked, while others had to have ears that flopped. In America (but not now in Britain), dogs' ears are sometimes cropped to make them look pricked and menacing. From time to time rules are revised.

There is something a little chilling in our godlike abilities to form and shape dogs, adjusting them to accord with our fashionable ideas of how they should look. Until recently, similar skin color and other rules (as rigid as those of dog breeding) were an important part of socially acceptable love between humans.

Some canine characteristics have been bred to a point of refinement that is detrimental to the dogs themselves. Dalmatians, with their lovely even spots, are prone to hereditary deafness. German shepherds, bred to creep menacingly on low hindquarters, often suffer from hip displacement. Great Danes and Newfoundlands have bodies too big for their hearts, and usually live short lives. The more we accentuate a breed's peculiarities, the more it's apt to become a disability. Some people say the same of the human brain.

Nowadays some breeders are making new crosses of favorite dogs that have been overly interbred. There is a new poodle-Labrador mix, and a rottweiler-Labrador too. With these deliberate mixes one is reminded of the story of George Bernard Shaw, who was approached by a beautiful woman (traditionally Isadora Duncan, although Shaw himself said it was not she), suggesting they make together a child with her beauty and his brains. Shaw replied, "But what if the child turned out to have my body and your brains?"

WHEN LUGGS WAS with me and I was in charge of the small things of his life, brushing him, giving him food, taking him for walks, I was getting a better hold on life, both Beth's and mine. Luggs didn't care about his illustrious pedigreed ancestry. His main concern was everyday life, for, though Paul had proudly told me that his dog had "papers" and could have been shown, Luggs was a jolly, pedestrian character. Show dogs have to walk sedately and stand erectly still while judges examine their minutest qualities. Luggs was found to be too friendly and inquisitive (even for a Labrador) to adjust to that life, so instead of a luminous "career," he was given up for adoption as a pet, and subsequently cheered us all.

Dogs, family dogs, represent a happy world of bones and treats and country walks. In spite of our manipulation of them, any dog, mongrel or pedigreed, can give us what dogs give best: enthusiasm for daily life. T. H. White, author of *The Sword in the Stone,* told how he casually acquired a beautiful red setter to "go with" his fancy motor car and top hat. "I felt," he wrote, "that 'the dog' would suit me nearly as nicely as the hat did." He didn't expect to change and fall in love with Brownie herself. When she died, neither his fine car nor his hat consoled him. White went to Dublin and "kept myself drunk for a week."

Although we still had Ruffy, when Peter was in kindergarten we adopted a little dog called Rosie. Peter was a gentle child who loved flowers, and he named Rosie, though she was unflower-like and of many mixes. Rosie was black, fat, and, even to those who loved her, not noble of aspect. She loved children and food. Or perhaps food first, and then children. But there was never a child who came to our house who did not love Rosie. Long after she died, college graduates revisiting our house after years of absence, big men whom I remembered as dear little boys, would ask, "What happened to Rosie?"

Little animals, unlike little children, did not love Rosie. She even learned to hunt frogs. She would sit motionless by the pond for hours, and then pounce. We were distressed by this, because we liked having frogs in our pond. Richard sternly told Rosie she was an "undog," but she didn't seem to care or mend her ways. So Richard attached a bell to her collar to warn the frogs as she sprang. It worked pretty well, but she remained fat, doubtless discovering other small creatures to catch and eat. She grew thin and lame in old age but lived to eighteen, so her diet must have suited her! She was eventually found drowned in the same pond where she stalked frogs. Maybe she was trying to get just one more before she died.

AFTER SHE BECAME ill, Beth, who had been so elegant and fashionably dressed, seemed to wear the same pair of old brown pants every time I saw her. Of course she did. She had lost all her hair and had had a double mastectomy. In previous times she used to urge me to go shopping, used to compliment me whenever my outfit "matched" (which it seldom did). She herself had been groomed and calm, smart but conventional.

But after Beth had cancer, I found myself looking for compliments to make on her appearance, cheerily asking *her* what she would be wearing whenever she told me she was going somewhere. One day she arrived in a pair of new, rather heavy shoes.

"Do my shoes look silly?" she asked me anxiously. It startled me. I had never thought of her asking my opinion, or caring about it either. It turned out that she was having trouble with her feet. The chemotherapy had given her a sense of permanent pins and needles.

"No, they look wonderful. All the young women are wearing shoes just like that. They're right in fashion," said I. I had noticed my son's girlfriend in a pair of stout shoes, but a lesser authority on fashion than myself would have been hard to find.

"I'm glad you like them," she said. She looked hard at me, and neither of us said any more.

Nature and Nurture

AFTER HER TREATMENTS, Beth took time off. She and her husband went on trips, once even to Italy, and Luggs stayed with us. It was then that I realized Beth had shared her life with me. She had allowed me to know her dog. When she was away, for her other clients she was just absent, but I still had her dog.

Luggs had become a member of our family as well as Beth's. The children gave him bones at Christmas and took him for walks when I was busy. Richard always took him out last thing at night for his evening "pee-rade." Peter took Luggs skating once. It was a funny sight to see this very tall young man dragging a rigid black dog across the icy pond. Luggs stood firmly, seeming to enjoy being pulled along. It was good for us all to have a new member of the family, especially such a clumsy, affectionate character. He enjoyed being with us, but was like a cousin who seldom visited, and found our ways a little odd. Although eager to please, he simply couldn't get the point of skating. Barbecues, needless to say, he understood.

For myself I began to believe that Beth would be well again. She would be away having a good time, and would tell me all about it when she returned. I in turn would tell her what Luggs had been doing with us. Paul even sent us a postcard, including his "love to Luggs," from Italy. While they were abroad we strode the fields joyously, the dogs and I. Mary Russell Mitford wrote about her dog, Marmion,

> Who dreamed of death that gazed on thee?
> Thy light and golden form
> Skimming along the meadowy sea,
> A sunbeam in the storm.

Yes, it's hard to have dark fears around a dog joyfully scampering across the fields, intent on nothing but delight.

I talked to Luggs when Beth wasn't around. He would respond to my chatter, wagging his tail enthusiastically: "Do you miss your mom *(wag, wag)*? Even if you don't, I do. She'll be back on Thursday *(wag, wag)*. Do you miss your real mom, your dog mom? *(wag, wag)*. I miss my mom, too. It's a funny world, isn't it, Luggs? What does it all *mean*, Luggsey boy?"

Between these "conversations," there would be pauses on his part to lick up deer scat (his particular treat) or defecate (which he did discreetly, turning his back to me). He flopped down patiently for *my* pauses, usually to pick flowers or berries. It seems we understood each other's habits well enough. It was hard to tell whether our hopes and fears jibed as well. Did Luggs find picking flowers as hard to understand as I found gulping feces?

In the eighteenth century, Descartes appeased many people's consciences by "proving" that the difference between animals and men was that animals could not communicate their thoughts, and thus lacked reason. So, although fascinating and complicated, they were only machines, and could not feel. Treating them badly was not at all the same as mistreating a human.

An opponent of Descartes, Jeremy Bentham, pointed out that putting a "Dog Machine" next to a "Bitch Machine" would surely result in a "Puppy Machine," but try that with two mechanical watches and see what happens! Dogs must therefore be "higher" than machines. But, said Jeremy Bentham, "The question is, not Can they [animals] *reason*? nor, Can they *talk*? but, Can they *suffer*?"

Although most people now believe that animals *can*

suffer, it doesn't always stop us from making them do so, and we still compare our perceptions and abilities with those of other animals, including dogs, and still try to sort the basic differences between us.

In *Travels with Charley,* John Steinbeck wrote that his poodle Charley was a "first-rate dog and has no wish to be a second-rate human." Although Steinbeck chatted constantly to Charley as they traveled together across America, he never talked down to him in baby talk, which Charley, he said, disdained.

In the 1700s William Cowper wrote two poems exploring the nature of his dog, Beau. The British poet was on a walk one day when he saw a beautiful water lily in a pond. He tried, and failed, to reach it, so he continued to walk. To his astonishment, Beau jumped into the water, retrieved the water lily, and "dropped / The treasure at my feet." Cowper wrote "Beau and the Waterlily," commemorating the event:

"The world," I cried,
"Shall hear of this thy deed:
My dog shall mortify the pride
Of man's superior breed."

A strange tale, that of a dog picking flowers. But Beau also had his doggy nature. So we have another poem by Cowper called "Beau and the Bird":

But you have killed a tiny bird,
Which flew not till to-day,
Against my orders, whom you heard
Forbidding you the prey.
Nor did you kill that you might eat,
And ease a doggish pain,
For him, though chased with furious heat,
You left where he was slain.

Then the poet wrote "Beau's Reply":

Sir, when I flew to seize the bird,
In spite of your command,
A louder voice than yours I heard,
And harder to withstand.

Finally the dog says to the writer (and I too have to wonder about this one),

If killing birds be such a crime
(Which I can hardly see),
What think you, sir, of killing time
With verse addressed to me?

Freud's friend Marie Bonaparte said her dog Topsy was wiser than herself. Topsy "simply inhales the scented June air, whilst I strive laboriously to trace vain signs on this paper." And who, she asks, "will read Homer or

Shakespeare when there are no more human eyes?" She was writing just before the Holocaust and World War II. At least we can still read about Topsy.

Dogs, like people, can have separate personalities in different circumstances. Savage police dogs will go home to their handler's family to be cuddled by little children. Guide dogs, once out of their harness, will frolic in the same park where they sedately kept to pathways. Dogs concentrate on their different sides with such focus, it's hard to tell which is their true nature.

Robin had been so full of fun and wit, and that is how I remember him best. But that hadn't saved him from the darkest end. All of us can howl in the black night and frivolously giggle at breakfast time. We try, sometimes with the help of therapy, to reconcile our diverse selves, or even to rid ourselves of our darker natures. We try learning to behave like a more acceptable personality, much as we teach a dog to resist barking or chasing cars. Our darker sides worry us, and can get us into trouble. We would feel better with a comfortably unified personality, with more light than darkness in our natures.

As a very small child I was given a doll constructed so that it had a smiling head and a crying head, one or the other hidden under a large skirt. You flipped the skirt to reveal whichever head you wished, and the opposite head remained like legs under the long skirt. I still remember screaming in terror when that doll was given to me by a well-meaning friend of the family. I think she might even have sewed it for me. Many years later, my mother reminded me that they had to take the doll away, *throw* it away into a trash can and close the lid, before I could be calmed.

Sometimes I used to wonder what our relationship would have been if Beth and I had lived in some poor village. Was her counseling a learned skill, or was it her very nature? She loved to hear about the Italian village where I once had lived, where we women did our laundry together, side by side, and soothed each other's sorrows while we scrubbed. In Italy I had never needed the kind of help I sought from Beth, but would life's experiences have trained her well enough to have counseled me had she not been a professional? There were always a few women in the village on whose calm wisdom the others leaned. Can village life replace the need for counseling?

I wasn't about to give up my American washing machine, and I doubt if, even before she became ill, Beth would have been interested in scrubbing her laundry by my side as a therapeutic exercise for both of us. So we sat and talked instead. I have no way of knowing what was her training and what was a sympathy between us.

Elizabeth Barrett, who had described her brothers'

three dogs as "an odious bloodhound," "the ugliest dog in all Christendom," and an unpleasing mastiff "who glories in battle," was given *her* famous dog, Flush, by her friend Mary Russell Mitford. Even those who aren't "dog lovers" can love a dog (even those for whom therapy is suspect can love a therapist), and Elizabeth believed that only her dog understood his mistress's dreary life:

> This dog only, crept and wept,
> Next a languid cheek that slept,
> Sharing in the shadow.

Elizabeth fed Flush on sponge cake and macaroons, and tried to teach him to read and do math. When she was unable to teach him, she concluded "his soul has the sensitivities of an artist, hence he finds the mechanics of arithmetic both tedious and inconvenient." That Flush might be *unable* to comprehend the "mechanics" was apparently not acceptable! When Elizabeth eloped with Robert Browning, there was no question of leaving behind her dog. Robert Browning had to take the dog along with its mistress, but it's uncertain that the dog his wife called "dear pretty little Flushie" was the bright center of Browning's life too. Flush seemed to think, according to Robert Browning, that his new master had been created for "the special purpose" of looking after him.

Dogs and other animals seem to have instinctive wisdom, but cerebral wisdom seems harder to prove. Recent experiments at Harvard University found dogs performed better than wolves or chimpanzees at reading human clues about which of two containers held food. Debates still continue today as to how much apes, taught to speak in American sign language, are thinking like us. Some say they have hopes and fears too. Others that they fool us by "communicating" as we expect them to.

At the beginning of the twentieth century there was a famous case of a horse, known as Clever Hans, who was said to be able to count and do simple arithmetic, usually by "reading" problems from a card. Hans would tap out the right answer with his foot. Numerous experiments were conducted on Hans, and he always seemed to be able to answer the questions correctly, even if his handler was not present. The horse was hailed as an example of our ability to communicate with animals. Eventually however, it was discovered that Hans was not looking at the written cards at all but at those who presented the problems, and he was reacting to small, unconscious changes in their demeanor when the correct answer came up. If no one was present, or the questioner didn't know the answer, Hans would tap his hoof randomly. This discovery was a disappointment to some people, but it still showed that animals often correctly "read" us. A dog that seems to sympathize with a tale of woe may be reacting with genuine feeling, but perhaps to the teller rather than the tale itself.

Dogs have their own instinctive laws. When Luggs first arrived at our house, it was understood that he was in Nemo's territory. Indoors Nemo permitted Luggs to sleep on his bed until Nemo himself arrived, and then Luggs would get up casually and stroll to his own bed. The two dogs understood each other. Occasionally, just to establish precedence, Nemo would take Luggs's bed from him, nonchalantly relinquishing it just after Luggs had settled elsewhere.

Their particular rules of behavior work well for dogs in the wild. Pariah dogs hang around villages and get what scraps they can. Those who study these dogs find they have quite a structured social system, and they certainly reproduce successfully. We have come a long way in the short time (evolutionarily) since some dogs first crept around villages to join our lives. Few of us could live in the wilderness, and many dogs couldn't either. They, like us, would be "bewildered," which means being lost in the wilderness.

Dogs that have accompanied humans into what we think of as civilization have problems of their own. Like latchkey children, they spend too much time alone. Like many of us, they lack exercise and are overweight. They get used to luxury. Some people give their dogs birthday parties, complete with Frosty Paws ice cream. There are canine play groups and day care centers and beauty parlors. Dog toys, anniversary gifts, and all the other paraphernalia to fit dogs into our human world are big business.

Civilization, though, can make "clients" of us all. These days dogs sometimes even have counselors of their own. Like their human caretakers they get stressed and can't understand what the world wants of them. Some dogs, like some humans, take antidepressants to help them through their lives. But there is no legal bond in the love of people for dogs, and a dog is still property. The majority of puppies adopted by American families as pets are not kept for life. They can end up in pounds, or laboratories, or if nobody wants them they are subject to euthanasia. If wild dogs gaze longingly at the warmth of lighted windows on cold nights, would they prefer the ice cream parties and the Prozac?

WHEN BETH FIRST returned to work after her chemotherapy treatment, I didn't see her regularly, and she still looked thin and tired. When I did see her, as a diversion for us both, I sometimes told her stories. Stories of my childhood, stories of my life in Italy, stories of my neighbors or my friends. Stories I hoped to write.

One time I said I didn't feel much like talking.

"That would be a pity," Beth had said. She paused. "You're the high point of my week."

So I told her more stories. She told me she would have liked to be a writer.

"Sitting in front of unwritten pages all day, trying to reach a world outside that can't respond? At least until you've almost forgotten your message to it."

"But how nice to leave a book behind," said she.

"Think of yourself," I said to Beth. "You perform the same function as a writer, but in reverse. You sit, and the outside world comes to you, bringing you contact. A writer sits and reaches out to the outside world. It's the same profession in reverse."

I was thinking too of how a writer steps back from the world to get it in focus. Had Beth been trying to teach me to do that with my own life? Had talking to her somewhat untangled me from a net of grief? The grief was still there, but now, when I laughed with those I loved, or walked in the sunshine with the dogs, the knots of my despair, though still visible, were a little distance away from where I was.

"You leave behind changed lives," I said. "More than most writers."

"I hope so," she replied. Something about the way she spoke bothered me.

"Are you sure you're not working too hard? Are you sure you're quite well now? Are you *sure* you are all right?"

She laughed. "What a fusspot you are! Why don't you give worrying a rest? You always have to worry about something, don't you?" I laughed too.

"You thought you had a client, and you got a mother hen," I said.

Forgiveness

BETH'S HAIR GREW back, not gray but brown, and she slowly began to put on weight again. I do not know if she retained her other clients while her illness kept her away from her office for so long. I suspect not many, because as she began to work more regularly she would offer me a whole morning from which to choose my appointment. I still didn't pay for sessions, although by then we had more money and we could have done so. When I asked Beth about it, she said she preferred "our own arrangement."

Although she was working again, Beth still went away quite often, usually to visit family, and left Luggs with me for the weekend. I saw her pretty regularly now for an hour each week, but with Luggs I spent many hours. I know now that Beth was spending as much time as possible with her family but sometimes, less than half humorously, I used to grumble that I saw more of Luggs than of Beth.

"He's my surrogate," she would laugh. I did not laugh back. I loved Luggs, but I wanted no canine surrogates.

We were always happy, though, to talk about Luggs. It was a relaxed meeting place for us. Her children were grown and Luggs was obviously an important member of their family, into which I now got even more glimpses. She told how he stole her Mother's Day chocolates. She told how the vet had said he was too fat, and how hard it was for Paul to resist feeding him. How he was "helping" Paul dig a new pond in their back garden. She told me about Luggs and Paul collecting golf balls together on a nearby golf course. It seemed that the golf club wasn't interested in getting the balls back, so Paul put a notice in the local post office and sold them. First, Beth told me, laughing, Paul graded and sorted them carefully. He took his golf ball business "very seriously," she chuckled. It was nice to talk about ordinary daily things. Too often I had pressed her to clarify for me the meaning of life, a hard task even for a saint!

As Beth became even stronger, our relationship grew more professional again. She seemed to insist on it, as if it were proof to her of her recovery. But I, of course, could not forget that she had had cancer. The presence of her illness was there still, crouched down between us like a great gloomy hound of despair. Sometimes, when we laughed and chatted, it crawled under the table. Then I might notice that Beth sank rather too gratefully into her sofa, or that she looked distracted. There between us would be sitting once more the dark, solid body of my anxiety.

Once I had asked Beth if she had ever considered bringing Luggs to her therapy sessions; she said she was afraid he might "bother" her clients. I suspected she felt more able to manage the rhythm of her practice without him.

Freud did not feel this way. His chow Jofi was always with him, even attending sessions with his patients (at that time they were not called clients). Freud justified his dog's presence, claiming that his patients seemed more relaxed, sometimes seeming able to tell the dog what they otherwise could not express. Jofi would lie close to the couch, where a particularly depressed patient could touch her for comfort. Freud described how, at the end of fifty minutes, Jofi would stand up and yawn, indicating that the session was over!

Beth didn't have Jofi (or Luggs) in her office, but she

was very good at smoothly ending sessions, gliding out of her chair and over to her desk after exactly forty-five minutes, without ever seeming to glance at her watch. I used to think of her skill enviously when guests stayed too long at our house, but also resented it because it *was* a skill. I wanted Beth, like my mother or my sister, to say, "Do you really have to go?"

THE BIRTHDAYS OF my dead were always a hard time. Every season seemed to have one, to be awaited with dread. Robin's was in spring, Anna's in the summer. It was strange that at the saddest times, on their birthdays, I would remember most their laughter. Anna, laughing with me when the potatoes burned. Robin, rocking with tears of delight when his brother pretended to spear a Jell-O rabbit I had made for Easter dinner.

We talked about Anna and Robin, but of course Beth knew I was talking about her as well.

"*I* am learning to live in the present," she said. "You are going to have to do that too. Think of life like half a glass of water. Is the glass half full, or half empty?"

"Depends if you drank half, or spilled half. Or only filled it halfway up in the first place," said I pettishly. It wasn't the first time I had heard about the glass.

Beth had always been convinced that I must be angry,

angry at Robin, angry at fate, now even angry with her for becoming ill. She was apologetic on the rare times we talked about her illness, or when she had to interrupt her routine with medical matters.

In the past she had maneuvered me into complaining and "expressing my anger," as she put it. She had always been the mother dog, allowing, even encouraging, liberties of expression, inviting me to attack, to bite and worry her tail with my sharp milk teeth, and then forgiving me. But puppies, like children, lose their baby teeth, and with their second teeth come new rules about biting.

"Why do the people I love always die?" I wailed. "There must be something about me. I only have to love someone and they die."

Beth wasn't fooled. She looked at me hard. "You haven't got that kind of power," she said firmly, very firmly. "You can't make people die or live."

Ashamed, I realized what I had really been saying.

"I'm so sorry," I said.

"Don't be." She smiled. "But you have had bad luck. If you like to call it that." As usual she looked so worried and concerned about *me* that I wanted to cry. This time I didn't.

It wasn't only anger. Beth talked about "forgiveness" as well. Whom was I supposed to forgive? Robin? Anna? God? Or perhaps myself. Forgiveness is complicated, at least for most humans. The easiest way was to take the blame of fate on my own shoulders. Absurd little incidents would haunt me, the silliest being the time when I gave Robin one of Peter's baby teeth in a sandwich.

In our house the tooth for the fairy was always put into a sandwich bag under the pillow. That way the tooth fairy could find it, she having learned the hard way how impossible it is to find a single tiny tooth under the pillow of a sleeping child. Little Peter, having lost a tooth, had collected his dues, and there was a sandwich bag in the middle of the counter where I made sandwiches. That morning was a rushed one. Robin was hurrying to catch a train to Philadelphia, and I made him a sandwich to take for lunch. It wasn't until midday that I remembered, with horror, I had used the bag lying on the counter for his sandwich. I urgently called Robin.

"Don't eat the sandwich. Peter's tooth is in it." Too late. He had already bitten down on his brother's tooth. For once he wasn't amused, and he never accepted a sandwich from me again. For some obscure reason, I never could forgive myself. After he died, I would wake at 4 A.M. and remake that sandwich, again and again putting it into a fresh bag. I suppose it represented for me all the mistakes I had made, all the things I had done wrong that had allowed my son to die.

Because he thought he had allowed his own son to die, Llywelyn, a thirteenth-century Welsh king, acted impulsively. Llywelyn went out to battle, leaving the dog, Gelert, with his baby son. When he returned he couldn't find his son, but only Gelert, lying covered in blood. Llywelyn immediately concluded that the dog had killed the baby, and in a blind rage he killed the dog, who lay there weakly, unable to defend itself. Immediately afterward, as the story goes, he found his son, next to the body of a huge wolf killed by the gallant Gelert. In some of the versions the child is old enough to ask for his doggy friend. In others he is merely found safely cooing under an upturned cradle. In all the versions, Llywelyn never forgives himself for blaming his dog. He cries to Heaven in remorse, and builds the dog a costly tomb. But his remorse does live on, because centuries later, we still remember it.

We remember Isaac Newton more for his theory of gravity than for his dog. But he could forgive with greatness too, and once he had to forgive his dog. Newton was devoted to his Pomeranian, named Diamond. Just before he was ready to publish his theory of gravity, Newton left Diamond in his study while he went to answer the door. Diamond was disturbed by the sound of voices but couldn't get out of the room, and frantically ran around barking, hitting the table with a lighted candle on it. Obeying the laws of gravity, the candle fell over, and Newton's papers, his work of years, were completely burned.

"Oh Diamond, Diamond," he is reported to have cried, "thou little knowest what damage thou hast done." In a remarkable example of forgiveness, he lifted the dog into his arms and did not punish her. He wrote, "Because of Diamond I have had to begin much of the work afresh. . . . She knew not what she was doing. . . . Her place remains at my side or against my feet when I lie abed." It was another year before he could present his theory of gravity to the scientific world.

Dogs themselves will forgive humans unconditionally. They don't seem to wrestle with problems of blame, remaining steadfastly loyal to their own natures, and to us. Children as well are as quick as puppies to forgive, although psychologists might claim they bury hurts like bones in their own memories, to be muddily retrieved years later.

Loss

ONE DAY I ARRIVED at Beth's office and saw that her bookcase was empty.

"What happened to your books?" Then I noticed the pictures were down too. "Where are your pictures?" I suppose there was panic in my voice. She laughed.

"Oh, I decided to sell my office. I didn't feel like bothering to run the building anymore."

"You mean you are retiring?" (Of course that was not what I meant).

"No, no. I just don't own the whole building anymore. I'm renting a little room now. In the basement."

Soothing, logical, intelligent. She even took me downstairs to see the new "office" in the basement.

"It's got no windows!" I cried.

"*I* think," she said firmly, "it's a lovely office. I'm enjoying having fewer responsibilities. Now when would you like to come next week?"

I was halfway home before I decided to turn around. When I got back to her office Paul was there, moving books.

"I came back to help you," I said. Rather than moving books herself, Beth was sitting on the leather sofa, eating the contents of the basket I had brought.

"You don't have to do this," she said.

"But I want to help you."

Beth didn't get up but watched as Paul and I worked. I carried books and stacked them neatly in the bookcase in the new office. Books on all the psychological possibilities you could imagine. Books that at the moment I deeply distrusted, as (in spite of what she said) I distrusted everything else. But I had an instinct. So I hauled books.

Very shortly before my sister Anna had died, I had asked what I "could do for her." She thought for a moment, and then asked me to hem her living room curtains as she did not "feel up to doing it" herself. So I, who longed to help her face the unknown, sat with her silently and hemmed curtains. It was what she had wanted me to do.

I do not know if Beth was afraid of death. All I know was that she was not interested in talking about her own mortality to me (who so feared losing her). But even those who so ably comfort our fears must have their own fears too.

When Freud was dying from cancer of the jaw (he smoked cigars), he wanted the comfort of his dog on his bed beside him. Freud had dreaded aging, and it seems he also feared death. He had always hated celebrating his birthday, so his daughter used to have his birthday parties with their three dogs. Everybody, including the dogs, wore paper hats, and the dogs were offered the first slices of birthday cake. Freud would be presented with a poem, hanging in an envelope around the neck of its ostensible author, one of the dogs. Freud's daughter would then read the poem aloud for the canine bard.

That a dog's acknowledgment of Freud's aging could have been acceptable to Freud, while a human's was not, is curious. It seems to me an evasion of reality. But perhaps he could more easily admit a recognition of mortality to dogs, because dogs, as far as we know, do not dwell on such things.

Our dog Rabbit, the one who erred in the desert, seemed to have a simple enough philosophy. Like most of her kind, smells were her delight. She ate with enthusiasm, wagged her tail eagerly, and loved us more than we deserved. It was impossible to imagine her harboring dark thoughts of mortality. But I wonder still about her perception of her own death.

One morning we couldn't find Rabbit. We searched for her and finally discovered her lying at the very back of the doghouse. No guilty look, no tail wagging. She just lay there. I took her to our vet, and, after examining her, he said gently that there was nothing he could do. She was dying. We could have her "put down," or bring her home. She was not in pain, so I decided to bring her home. We put her back where she had chosen to be, in the doghouse. She lay there for a week. Each morning we expected to find her dead. Sometimes she would slightly move her tail in a whispered wag. Sometimes her ears would prick when we said her name. We thought of moving her or taking her back to the vet, but there was something about the way she looked at us that made us leave her there.

Then we had snow. We covered the whole doghouse with thick tarpaulins to keep out the cold, and she wagged her tail a bit when we tucked her in. The next morning, she was gone. We didn't believe it. She hadn't touched food or water for over a week and hadn't seemed strong enough to stand, much less walk. We searched for her, looking for footprints in the fast-falling snow, poking into briar patches hung with icicles, tangling our hair in the freezing brush. We didn't find her. She had not intended that we should.

It was not until the following spring, when all the snow had melted, that we found her body beyond the pond. She was lying under the tree where long ago she had stolen all those eggs.

When our dogs die it breaks our hearts, and, since their expected life span is about a seventh of a human's, they never live long enough. Barring the unexpected, unless you are old, to get a dog is to get a friend who will surely die before you. Rudyard Kipling put it this way in "The Power of the Dog":

There is sorrow enough in the natural way
From men and women to fill our day;
And when we are certain of sorrow in store,
Why do we always arrange for more?
Brothers and Sisters, I bid you beware
Of giving your heart to a dog to tear.

ONE OF THE most famous dogs of all time was Nipper, the pet terrier of a nineteenth-century painter, Francis Barraud. Nipper (named because he nipped people's heels) had belonged to Barraud's brother, Mark, who had died. Barraud owned a phonograph, and one day he noticed that Nipper seemed puzzled by "where the voice came from." In 1895 (although by then Nipper too had died), Barraud remembered Nipper in a portrait he called *A Dog Looking at and Listening to a Phonograph*. The Royal Academy turned down the painting. Barraud offered it to the Edison Bell Company, which also turned it down because "Dogs don't listen to phonographs." Then, in 1899, Barraud's painting was accepted by the newly formed British Gramophone Company, on condition that the artist alter the painting to depict the company's make of gramophone. Barraud altered the painting, for which he received fifty pounds, and he was paid fifty more pounds for the copyright. In 1907, "His Master's Voice" became the company's trademark, recognized worldwide.

The intently listening dog was a charmingly winning image for many people. I, myself, see something more: a dog trying to connect with a vanished master, as I, too, have yearned to connect with those who are no longer here.

Comfort

AFTER SHE MOVED into her new office I didn't see Beth for several weeks. First I went away, and then she went away. We had an appointment the day after she returned. I made soup. Not vegetarian soup, but real chicken soup, using a whole chicken. I collected flowers.

The chicken, however, had died in vain, at least as far as Beth was concerned. She canceled the appointment the night before, saying she had "a viral infection." She would call again when she was well.

I waited. A week passed, and then two more. Finally I called *her*. Yes, she would see me the next day.

I waited down in the basement with more chicken

soup, chocolates, and flowers. She arrived and came very slowly down the steps, clinging to the banister. I had never seen her so thin, and her color was terrible.

"You don't look well." She sat down at once, without removing her coat. They had done their best with the new little office. There were pictures on the walls and the same cushions and stuffed animals on the sofas. A fluffy toy rabbit had fallen onto the floor, so I picked it up and settled it in the corner of the sofa. It was hard not to think that the windowless little office, with its hangings and artifacts, looked a bit like an elaborate tomb.

"This virus has knocked me silly," said Beth.

"There's been a lot of flu about," said I. We were both silent.

"As long as it isn't the cancer," I said. She sat there, looking at her hands. She had had lovely skin, but it was now grayish. Of course I knew what she was going to say.

"I'm sorry," she said, "I'm afraid it is. But I'm on chemo again. I've not given up."

There we were again, not giving up. We talked about the chemo, her doctor. I talked about the survivors I knew, the "list of survivors" I kept in my bag of hope.

"And I have some exciting news too," she said. "I'm getting a new dog."

A new dog. What about Luggs? What did she mean "a new dog"?

"Is Luggs all right? What's happened to Luggs?" I suppose I thought that the whole world was dying again. Luggsey. Darling, clumsy Luggs. Beth, ill but still professional, immediately saw my panic.

"No, no, he's fine. I'm getting a little lap dog. I've always wanted a lap dog. I wanted a little dog when we got Luggs, but Paul liked Luggs."

I had always known really that Luggs was Paul's dog. It didn't matter now. I had started by loving Luggs for Beth. Now I loved him anyway.

If she was getting a new dog, surely it meant that she was going to live? She wouldn't, I thought, want to adopt a dog if she weren't. But she looked so ill, and there was something so uncharacteristic about her wanting a toy dog at all. What could she want with a silly little dog? Of course it was comfort she needed.

She asked if I could sometimes care for the new dog along with Luggs, and I agreed. "Long term," she said, looking at me rather hard, her sister would take it. She didn't need to explain. Later I wondered, though, what she had really tried to tell me.

The next visit she looked even sicker, and she had the new dog in the office with her. It was a tiny Yorkshire terrier, and had its pink calico bed on the sofa beside her. She told me it weighed six pounds, and was called Pretzel. It was a male. I had never seen such a small dog before. He sat on Beth's knee, and she patted him tenderly.

Of course I was anxious to love him; any friend of hers was a friend of mine. I had even become quite fond of the floppy toy rabbit she kept on her sofa, complete with pink apron and bonnet. Once I would have wondered why she had such a silly toy, she with her degrees and doctorate! Later I realized that sometimes we all need childlike comfort, from wherever it might come. If fluffy rabbits were part of her office, even they had become dear to me.

I called Pretzel over. He came, and jumped on my lap. I had expected him to be rather floppy like a soft toy, but he was surprisingly muscular, and snuggled onto my lap with a good deal of strength.

What about Luggs? He apparently accepted but took little notice of Pretzel. He knew, as dogs do, that Pretzel might be the size of a large rat, but was another dog, and therefore to be treated as such. Canine laws applied, and although Luggs could have swallowed Pretzel in one mouthful, he was not legally swallowable, being one of his own kind.

I found this out pretty soon, because only a few days after I had met Pretzel, Beth went to New York to see a specialist, and I got to have both the dogs. Nemo, who could have eaten Pretzel in *half* a mouthful, simply sniffed him all over and walked away. Both big dogs had clearly decided to ignore him.

Pretzel didn't mind. Although, way back, his ancestors were ratting terriers, all he had left of that legacy was luxuriant golden bangs (which originally would have kept flying dirt out of terriers' eyes as they scrabbled for rats). Pretzel bonded with nobody but humans with laps, and it didn't seem to matter much to whom the lap was attached. *In extremis* he would accept a cushion instead of a lap, but otherwise every time I sat down he jumped up. That was about all he did. Occasionally I took him for a tiny scamper on the lawn, all the while looking out for hawks, which wouldn't have shared the dogs' scruples about making a nice little meal of him. At night he whimpered unless his pink basket was carried right upstairs and set beside the bed. In the car he sat on my knee. Like a hunting dog or a police dog he knew his job, and his job was human laps.

At least for those who sit a lot, small lap dogs have been popular for centuries. In Europe, from about the fourteenth century onward, lap dogs, mostly small spaniels and Pomeranians, became popular with the rich and noble, especially women. In those days most noblewomen gave up their babies almost at once to wet nurses. Little dogs were ideal, kindly companions and could be cuddled like babies. Contemporaries called them "Rubbing dogs," or "Comforters."

It was also thought (according to Dame Juliana Barnes, the fifteenth-century prioress of England's Sopwell Nunnery), that "small ladyes poppees . . . bere awaye the fleas." In addition, wrote John Caius, who besides writing on dogs was also the Royal physician, "they ease the pain of the stomach, being often applied to it, or frequently born in the bosom of the diseased person, by the moderation of their vital heat. Moreover it is believed from their sickness and frequently their [the dog's] death that diseases even are transferred to them, as if the evil passed over to them owing to the intermingling of vital heat."

I told Beth about the fleas, which amused her, but I didn't tell her about the transmission of disease. Little Pretzel was bred for kindly comfort. Like any true dog he would have done whatever was expected of him. I am sure that had it been required of him, he would have taken on Beth's disease itself.

NOT LONG AFTER her visit to the specialist, Beth made another appointment with me. I waited outside her office. When she arrived I could see that she was walking with difficulty. I took her bag, and we went down to the basement together. She smiled and asked how *I* was. I noticed, not for the first time, that her speech was a little slurred. I asked how she was. She was pleased, she said, because the doctor in New York had said she should "take a rest" from more chemotherapy. I was silent.

"You could come to the house for appointments instead of here," she said, speaking very slowly. I said that would be fine. I had just realized that, of course, the slurred speech was because she was taking morphine.

We were silent for a while. I fiddled with the white toy rabbit. Finally she spoke.

"You know, you might want to get a backup. In case there are days when I can't see you." She looked at me so kindly.

"What kind of backup?"

"Another counselor. Just in case I don't feel well. I don't want to feel you can't get help."

"There isn't another counselor," I said. "There'll never be another. There isn't anybody like you, that I would love." I couldn't see her across the room because I was crying. Really crying.

"I'm sorry I'm crying. I didn't mean to," I said.

"I'm sorry I'm crying too," she said. She was. We sat there.

Suddenly she said, "I'm afraid I'm going to throw up." There was a basin under the sofa; apparently she kept it there for the purpose. I helped her, and cleaned up.

"I'll take you home," I said. She rose slowly.

"Do I get a hug?" she said. She seemed suddenly so small and so forlorn. I hugged her. There wasn't much of her now, she was so thin.

"Not so hard," she said, "because of the pain."

We locked the door behind her, and somehow I got her home. After I got home, I remembered I had left a vase of fresh flowers on her table. She never went back to the office. And I avoided driving past it, taking another route.

I WENT TO SEE Beth at her house. She was in the living room, in a hospital bed. I had brought her a large red poppy, which I put beside the bed. I sat down beside her.

"I want to ask you something," I said. She nodded. "Would you like me to write about you? And Luggs."

She smiled. "I'm very touched," she said quietly. She closed her eyes and then opened them again. "I can't talk much," she whispered. As usual, though, she smiled as if nothing were wrong. I took her hand.

"You don't have to talk. Everything's been said," I replied.

I sat quietly, holding her hand. Both dogs were in the room, Pretzel in his pink basket, Luggs sniffing around Pretzel's empty food dish. I saw that Beth was trying to say something again. I bent my head so I could hear her.

"Thank you for being a friend," she whispered. There was a ghost of a smile again. "A *special* friend."

Luggs came over to me. He put his paw on my lap and rested his head against my knee. Pretzel didn't stir. He looked like a golden wig in an inverted pink pillbox hat. I patted Luggs, and then I took his paw in my free hand. I sat for a while holding his paw and her hand. Then Beth went to sleep, and I left.

Love

I DON'T KNOW WHY I dialed Beth's answering machine one more time, when I knew that she had died. A dog can listen to a recording of "His Master's Voice," and we can't blame him for confusing reality with expectation, but *I* should have known better. Maybe I was hoping for a miracle. Anyway, they had not yet disconnected the machine. Her voice was cheery, and clear as a bell:

"Hello. This is Dr. Beth Johnson. I'm not able to answer your call just now, but you can leave a message, taking as long as you like . . ."

As long as I liked? Well, I suppose I knew it had been a moment of weakness.

Paul called to ask if I could take Luggs the weekend of the funeral, because there would be "so many people" around. Then, afterward, he would be going away for a few weeks. So could I keep Luggs for a bit? Of course I could. What about Pretzel? Pretzel had already gone back to the dog home.

"But I thought her sister was to take him."

"Oh, no, there was never a question of that. Her sister travels too much. She can't have a dog."

No one had asked *me* if I would take him. I didn't say anything. What could I say? What had Beth intended? And why had she told me her sister would take Pretzel? At least I had something real to make me angry.

Luggs came. I wished I could have taken him to the funeral. I almost did, but I thought Paul wouldn't approve. So I went by myself. The church was packed. Both the hymns and the ministry concentrated a lot on eternal life, calling the service a "Celebration of Life."

I sat at the very back. Apart from recognizing her sisters, I didn't know anyone except Paul. There were so many people, and every one of them was a stranger to me. Yet we were all there because we had known her in our different ways. It was the kind of thing we would have talked about, she and I. How all the little pieces of a person are brought together at the funeral.

We would have talked about this, she and I, and probably argued, too. I would also have told her how I had to leave the funeral early, because I was embarrassed. I wasn't properly "celebrating" her life but whimpering forlornly. She would have listened.

When I was home, the dogs were exuberant to see me, and we went on a very long walkies. We went on our usual route. During the night some curious mushrooms had grown in the damp woods. They were pale, glowing pink, poking through the dark path. Luggs didn't even attempt to eat them.

When we got back, Richard was waiting.

"We may have Luggs quite a bit now. I hope you don't mind?"

"I know. I would have taken Pretzel too. If you had wanted."

"I know you would. And I love you."

"I love you too," he said.

Bibliography

My Therapist's Dog is a memoir and not intended as a reference book, but I am particularly indebted to the works of Stephen Budiansky, Stanley Coren, Katharine MacDonogh, and Mary Elizabeth Thurston, along with the other books mentioned below.

Ash, Edward C. *Dogs: Their History and Development.* 2 volumes. New York: Benjamin Blom, 1972.

Bekoff, Marc. *Minding Animals.* New York: Oxford University Press, 2002.

Budiansky, Stephen. *The Truth about Dogs.* New York: Viking, 2000.

Bonaparte, Marie. *Topsy: The Story of a Golden-Haired Chow.* New Brunswick, NJ: Transaction Publishers, 1994.

BIBLIOGRAPHY

Carson, Gerald. *Men, Beasts, and Gods.* New York: Charles Scribner's Sons, 1972.

Coppinger, Raymond and Lorna. *Dogs.* New York: Scribner, 2001.

Coren, Stanley. *The Intelligence of Dogs.* New York: Free Press, 1994.

———. *The Pawprints of History.* New York: Free Press, 2002.

———. *Why We Love Dogs.* New York: Free Press, 1998.

Derr, Mark. *Dog's Best Friend.* New York: Henry Holt and Co., 1997.

Evans, E. P. *The Criminal Prosecution and Capital Punishment of Animals.* London: Faber and Faber, 1987.

Gorwill, Sylvia. *The Hairless Dogs of the World.* Gorwill, 1987.

Grenier, Roger. Translated by Alice Kaplan. *The Difficulty of Being a Dog.* Chicago: University of Chicago Press, 2000.

Hastings, Hester. *Man and Beast in French Thought of the Eighteenth Century.* Baltimore: Johns Hopkins University Press, 1936.

Kete, Kathleen. *The Beast in the Boudoir.* Berkeley: University of California Press, 1994.

Leonard, Robert Maynard, ed. *The Dog in British Poetry.* London: David Nutt, 1893.

MacDonogh, Katharine. *Reigning Cats and Dogs.* New York: St. Martin's, 1999.

Masson, Jeffrey. *Dogs Never Lie about Love.* New York: Crown, 1997.

Rosenblum, Robert. *The Dog in Art.* New York: Abrams, 1988.

Rowan, Roy and Brooke Janis. *First Dogs.* Chapel Hill, NC: Algonquin Books of Chapel Hill, 1997.

Thomas, Keith. *Man and the Natural World.* New York: Pantheon Books, 1983.

Thurston, Mary Elizabeth. *The Lost History of the Canine Race.* Kansas City, MO: Andrews and McMeel, 1996.

Toland, John. *Adolf Hitler.* Garden City, NJ: Doubleday, 1976.

Tuan, Yi-Fu. *Dominance and Affection.* New Haven: Yale University Press, 1984.

Vesey-Fitzgerald, Brian. *The Domestic Dog.* London: Routledge and Kegan Paul, 1957.

DATE DUE

OCT 2 0 2004			
OCT 2 0 2004			
GAYLORD			PRINTED IN U.S.A.